The Big Story: One God

SPRING HARVEST

Equipping the Church for action

Also available in Braille and Giant Print

Copyright © 2006 Spring Harvest

Steve Chalke asserts the moral right to be identified as the author of this work.

Published by
Spring Harvest
14 Horsted Square
Uckfield
East Sussex TN22 1QG

First edition 2006

ISBN   1 899 78855 7

Acknowledgements
Unless stated otherwise, all Scripture quotations taken from the HOLY BIBLE,
NEW INTERNATIONAL VERSION.
Copyright ©1973, 1978, 1984 by International Bible Society.
Used by permission of Hodder and Stoughton Limited.
All rights reserved. "NIV" is a registered trade mark of International Bible
Society.
UK trademark number 1448790

Please note that the inclusion of a quotation or example in this book does not
imply endorsement by Spring Harvest.

Spring Harvest. A Registered Charity.

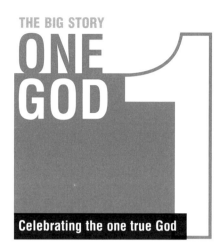

Spring Harvest 2006

STUDY GUIDE

by Steve Chalke

The author would like to express his thanks to the following, who have all made valuable contributions to the Spring Harvest 2006 Study Guide.

Theological editors: Mary Evans, Paul Gardner, Ernest Lucas, Derek Tidball, Chris Wright

Leadership Team: Pete Broadbent, Ian Coffey, Ruth Dearnley, Alan Johnson, Gerard Kelly, Jeff Lucas, Rachael Orrell

Over the next three years THE BIG STORY at Spring Harvest will investigate the themes of:

looking ahead

2006 –	ONE GOD
2007 –	ONE PEOPLE
2008 –	ONE HOPE

At Spring Harvest 2006 we begin by exploring THE BIG STORY: ONE GOD

Our FOUR DAILY THEMES shared by all age groups across the Event are:

contents

Each morning in THE BIG PICTURE we will study a key Bible passage as we trace the development of our theme through the Old and New Testaments which will enable us to grasp the understanding of God that scripture unfolds.

Day 2: From the Law –
Genesis 1:1–28

God, humanity, the cosmos and our place in it

Day 3: From the Histories and the Prophets –
1 Kings18:16–46

One universal God or many gods?

Day 4: From the Gospels –
Mark 2:1–12

Jesus – who did he think he was?

Day 5: From the New Testament Letters –
Ephesians 6:10–20

The ongoing battle, the powers and principalities

EVERY MORNING you also have the opportunity of being part of **THE BIG CONVERSATION**. With four distinct styles to choose from we invite you to investigate life's big questions in the light of God's Big Story – our task to understand God's map for life in his universe!

Radio 2:
Big, main stream, every day, relaxed, easy listening

Radio 4:
Probing, academic – a deeper analysis of key theological and cultural issues

Five Live:
Opinionated, investigative, interactive, participatory, headline driven

Edge FM:
Fast, edgy, multimedia, non-conformist, emerging culture

EACH AFTERNOON carefully selected speakers will probe one of the key issues arising out of the day's theme at a deeper level. Accessible but drawing on academic insights, **THE BIG QUESTION** will inform our thinking and affect our living.

BUT WE ARE NOT just here to learn – we are here to worship God. In fact, the hallmark of any true knowledge about God is that it will always lead to worship of God. So, under the name **THE BIG ENCOUNTER** our evening celebrations will engage with the theme of the day through the eyes, experience and songs of the psalmists.

Evening 2: Psalm 33
The lyrics of this wonderful Psalm affirm the power of God in creation, in governing history and in holding all people on earth to account for their actions. The whole universe comes from the creative word of the LORD.

Evening 3: Psalm 96
The writer of the psalm calls us to sing 'a new song' to the nations and to invite them to join in, for our God's song must be sung around the earth.

Evening 4: Psalm 22
Jesus died with the words of Psalm 22:1 on his lips. Whatever it was that led the original singer to pen these words, Jesus could identify with both their depths of anguish and heights of faith.

Evening 5: Psalm 42
Here the psalmist wrestles with the reality of evil and wickedness in a world that God is supposed to be running – but also wants to emphasise that his faith, trust and hope are in the LORD.

	morning	THEME	evening
	THE BIG PICTURE	**THE BIG CONVERSATION**	**THE BIG ENCOUNTER**
Pentateuch	Genesis	**Creator God**	Psalm 33
History	Kings	**Universal God**	Psalm 96
Prophecy			
Gospels	Mark	**Human God**	Psalm 22
Epistles	Ephesians	**Soveriegn God**	Psalm 42
Revelation			

This is our Big Story: Let's celebrate that our God is the God of the whole earth!

THE BIG STORY: ONE GOD

'The Lord our God, the Lord is one.'
Deuteronomy 6:4

Celebrating that our
God is the God of the
whole earth

INTRODUCTION

The tube train was as packed as usual as it trundled through central London. Most people were going about their business, oblivious to their travelling companions, but one young man had become preoccupied with the rather perplexed and obviously disorientated, foreign-looking, elderly gentleman sat opposite him. The elderly man kept looking down at a map of the Underground in the front of his diary then up at the maps displayed in the train and out of the window as the train passed through each station in turn. From time to time he'd scratch his head and sigh. Eventually the young man decided to go against the normal social code of travelling on the tube, approach the elderly gentleman and offer his assistance. Immediately his suspicions were confirmed, this man was not English – he was from Eastern Europe and on his first trip to the UK. Taking the diary that contained the map the young man stared at it, determined to locate exactly where they were. He didn't travel on the Underground very often, so was no expert himself. But turning the diary one way and then the other, he couldn't make head nor tail of it either. Finally, in frustration, he gave up and closed it and that's when he understood. The diary was French. The map inside its cover wasn't of the London tube at all – it was the Paris metro!

When you're on the London tube, with only a map of the Paris metro to guide you, you are going to get lost!

In his best-selling novel *Life After God*, Douglas Coupland freely admits he has no religious background. His book paints a stark, if often-humorous, picture of the seemingly purposeless nature of modern life. But it is his closing words that come as the biggest shock:

'Now – here is my secret: I tell it to you with an openness of heart that I doubt I shall ever achieve again, so I pray that you are in a quiet room as you hear these words. My secret is that I need God – that I am sick and can no longer make it alone. I need God to help me give, because I no longer seem to be capable of giving; to help me be kind, as I no longer seem capable of kindness; to help me love, as I seem beyond being able to love.'[1]

'The earth is the LORD's, and everything in it,' reads Psalm 24. If you're living in God's world and the only map you have to guide you ignores that fact, you are going to get lost! The richness of creation is lost on you. Life becomes a disappointing and barren experience. To live without God in God's world is to sentence yourself to stumble and blunder through life with no sense of direction and no real understanding of what surrounds you.

Many put their faith in a 'Big Story' of some sort. On the evidence of the world around them some choose to believe God exists and some choose to believe God that does not exist. But each and every one of us lives by faith. Christians believe that life's big story is explained through God's dealings with humanity as unpacked in the Bible and particularly through Jesus – the Word God.

And it's this Big Story that Spring Harvest will explore over the next three years.

Genesis 1:1–28

The Beginning

In the beginning God created the heavens and the earth. Now the earth was formless and empty, darkness was over the surface of the deep, and the Spirit of God was hovering over the waters.

And God said, "Let there be light," and there was light. God saw that the light was good, and he separated the light from the darkness. God called the light "day", and the darkness he called "night". And there was evening, and there was morning—the first day.

And God said, "Let there be an expanse between the waters to separate water from water." So God made the expanse and separated the water under the expanse from the water above it. And it was so. God called the expanse "sky". And there was evening, and there was morning—the second day.

And God said, "Let the water under the sky be gathered to one place, and let dry ground appear." And it was so. God called the dry ground "land", and the gathered waters he called "seas". And God saw that it was good.

Then God said, "Let the land produce vegetation: seed-bearing plants and trees on the land that bear fruit with seed in it, according to their various kinds." And it was so. The land produced vegetation: plants bearing seed according to their kinds and trees bearing fruit with seed in it according to their kinds. And God saw that it was good. And there was evening, and there was morning—the third day.

And God said, "Let there be lights in the expanse of the sky to separate the day from the night, and let them serve as signs to mark seasons and days and years, and let them be lights in the expanse of the sky to give light on the earth." And it was so. God made two great lights—the greater light to govern the day and the lesser light to govern the night. He also made the stars. God set them in the expanse of the sky to give light on the earth, to govern the day and the night, and to separate light from darkness. And God saw that it was good. And there was evening, and there was morning—the fourth day.

And God said, "Let the water teem with living creatures, and let birds fly above the earth across the expanse of the sky." So God created the great creatures of the sea and every living and moving thing with which the water teems, according to their kinds, and every winged bird according to its kind. And God saw that it was good. God blessed them and said, "Be fruitful and increase in number and fill the water in the seas, and let the birds increase on the earth." And there was evening, and there was morning—the fifth day.

And God said, "Let the land produce living creatures according to their kinds: livestock, creatures that move along the ground, and wild animals, each according to its kind." And it was so. God made the wild animals according to their kinds, the livestock according to their kinds, and all the creatures that move along the ground according to their kinds. And God saw that it was good.

Then God said, "Let us make man in our image, in our likeness, and let them rule over the fish of the sea and the birds of the air, over the livestock, over all the earth, and over all the creatures that move along the ground."

So God created man in his own image, in the image of God he created him; male and female he created them.

God blessed them and said to them, "Be fruitful and increase in number; fill the earth and subdue it. Rule over the fish of the sea and the birds of the air and over every living creature that moves on the ground."

The BIG ISSUE

Teaching Block 1

The Creator God: Faith and Science

1.1 God and the 'Big Bang'

1.2 Understanding creation

  1.2.1 Seven days

  1.2.2 Mind the gap

  1.2.3 Days of revelation

  1.2.4 What a difference a day makes

  1.2.5 Literary approach

1.3 Pick your battles

1.4 What is science?

1.5 What is theology?

QUESTION TIME

Teaching Block 2

The Creator God: The Goodness of Creation

2.1 The good Creator

2.2 God's universe

2.3 The creation myths

2.4 A good creation

2.5 An ordered creation

2.6 A diverse creation

QUESTION TIME

Teaching Block 3

The Creator God: Human Identity

3.1 What does it mean to be human?

3.2 Made in the image of God

3.3 The broken image

3.4 The royal image

3.5 God and hierarchy

3.6 God and the sexes

3.7 God and individualism

3.8 God and creativity

3.9 God and stewardship

QUESTION TIME

FURTHER READING

The BIG ISSUE

'The universe that we observe has precisely the properties we should expect if there is, at bottom, no design, no purpose, no evil and no good, nothing but blind, pitiless indifference,'[2] claims Richard Dawkins, the Charles Simonyi Professor of the Public Understanding of Science at Oxford University.

'The fact of the matter,' according to Quentin Smith, 'is that the most reasonable belief is that we came from nothing, by nothing and for nothing … We should … acknowledge our foundation in nothingness and feel awe at the marvellous fact that we have a chance to participate in this incredible sunburst that interrupts without reason the reign of non-being.'[3]

If they are right, any purpose we see in our world or our lives is one that we have imposed – in truth, we are simply lost in space. But if creation really is the work of a person, of God himself, then creation has intrinsic meaning and our lives can have a purpose within it.

From its first four words 'In the beginning God' the Bible leaves no room for doubt. In his book *Café Theology* Michael Lloyd explains, 'This one statement alone is utterly transformational of all that follows. Behind life, the universe and everything is a person. Creation is therefore pregnant with the possibility of relationship with the person who made it, and transforms the experience of our lives.'[4]

All art is self-revelatory – every artist tells us something about who they are through their work. So, in much the same way as you glean something about an author by reading their words, a painter by examining their picture or a poet by studying their poem, we can learn a huge amount about God just by considering the fact of his creation.

Today we explore what creation tells us about who God is and who we are. But before we do so, we need to look at the thorny issue of faith and science, and ask some basic questions:

- How did the universe begin?
- Which one is right – the Bible or science?
- Did God really make the world in six days?

Teaching Block 1: The Creator God: Faith and Science

1.1
God and the 'Big Bang'

When it comes to creation and science, even Christians are divided over the issues. One of the most contentious is the age of the universe.

Some believe that the universe and earth were created around six thousand years ago – in six days.

ARCHBISHOP USSHER DATES THE WORLD: 4004 BC

James Ussher (1581–1656), Archbishop of Armagh, Primate of All Ireland, and Vice-Chancellor of Trinity College in Dublin, was highly regarded in his day as a churchman and as a scholar. But, of his many works, his treatise on the chronology of the Bible has proved the most controversial and durable. Based on his study of Middle Eastern and Mediterranean history and the genealogies of Scripture, he established the first day of creation as Sunday 23 October 4004 BC. He then went on to calculate the dates of other key biblical events, concluding, for example, that Adam and Eve were driven from Paradise on Monday 10 November 4004 BC, and that the ark touched down on Mount Ararat on 5 May 1491 BC 'on a Wednesday'.

possible Big Crunch, our image of the universe today is full of strange sounding ideas, and remarkable truths.'[6]

The two views are irreconcilably opposed. On one side is the overwhelming weight of the vast majority of the scientific community who, although they often disagree amongst themselves about the details, present a united front against the concept of a young earth. On the other is a smaller group of 'Creationists', including a number of highly qualified scientists, who have come to the conclusion that science has misled us. We should, however, acknowledge that not all 'young earthers' agree with Archbishop Ussher's precise dating scheme, and prefer simply to estimate that the earth is a few thousand years old. We should also note that Christians have always held a range of opinions on how to understand the time frame of Genesis 1. As early as AD 391, in his commentary on Genesis, Augustine argued that

However, since the Enlightenment science has called the theory of a 'young earth' into serious question. The discovery of fossilised dinosaurs in the mid-nineteenth century seemed to suggest that the earth was much older than the Bible allowed – 6000 years was not long enough for an entire genus to thrive, become extinct and fossilise. In the twentieth century the field of astrophysics has also advanced the argument for a much older universe. This supports the theory of an explosion of energy, or 'Big Bang' around 13.7 billion years ago, an idea first put forward in the 1920s by Georges Lemaître, a Belgian priest. Though, as Bill Bryson points out in *A Short History of Nearly Everything*, 'these things are notoriously difficult to measure.'[5]

> **Does Genesis tell us how the universe was created, or do the scientists?**

the 'days' of creation were not literal but figurative. When Darwin published *The Origin of the Species* in 1859, Christians adopted differing views. From the very start Darwin's theories were supported by some Christians and opposed by others.

For many the debate comes down to a single question: does Genesis tell us how the universe was created, or do the scientists? Do we put our trust in the divinely inspired word of God or a scientific textbook? But are science and scripture really at odds with each other?

'This is probably the most remarkable discovery of modern cosmology', says Professor Stephen Hawking, on his official website. 'In less than a hundred years, we have found a new way to think of ourselves. From sitting at the centre of the universe, we now find ourselves orbiting an average-sized sun, which is just one of millions of stars in our own Milky Way galaxy. And our galaxy itself is just one of billions of galaxies, in a universe that is infinite and expanding … I want you to share my excitement at the discoveries, past and present, which have revolutionized the way we think. From the Big Bang to black holes, from dark matter to a

1.2
Understanding creation

There are many views on how to understand the creation account in Genesis chapters 1–3. In his book *God, The Big Bang and Stephen Hawking*, David Wilkinson, Wesley Research Lecturer in Theology and Science at Durham University, sets out what he sees as the five main theories out of which these variations grow.[7] These theories may be summarised as follows.

1.2.1
Seven days

The Genesis account is literal truth – a simple description of the way the world was created. Those who hold this position claim that the seven (or more precisely six) days of creation in Genesis are 'literal periods of 24 hours'. So it was that over the course of one calendar week God created the earth, the sun, moon and stars, trees and plants, the animals of land, water and air, and finally man before resting on the seventh day. This view, which is far from compatible with modern scientific understanding, is borne out of a desire to take the text of the Bible seriously.

Many people believe that Genesis 1–3 is a literal explanation of how the world came into being. However, critics of the six-day creation theory claim that holding Genesis as a literal account is counter-productive – and that it actually does damage to the scriptures simply because taking them literally is not the same thing as taking them seriously.

1.2.2
Mind the gap

In deference to the scientific claims of an 'old universe' the gap theory, which was first proposed during the nineteenth century by Scottish preacher Thomas Chalmers, argues for a significant pause or gap to be inserted between the first two verses of Genesis 1.

According to Chalmers, 'Verse 1 refers to the original creation, which could be billions of years old. However, the fall of Satan is responsible for bringing ruin and destruction upon the creation and verse 2 is translated as "The earth became formless and void". The rest of chapter 1 is thus a seven-day work not of creation but of reconstruction, which did happen thousands of years ago.'[8]

Originally Chalmers' theory won huge support for it seemed to allow both the theologians and the scientists to be right at the same time. However, today there are few biblical scholars who believe it is honest to translate Genesis 1:2 as Chalmers did. Furthermore, if there were such a potentially enormous time interval between Genesis 1:1 and Genesis 1:2,

it is difficult to explain why this is not mentioned in the text itself, if indeed, as the theory suggests, the idea of days was intended to be taken literally in the first place.

1.2.3
Days of revelation

Another attempt to explain the apparent discrepancy between the biblical account and modern scientific understanding, and the billions of years of earth history absent from the Bible, suggests that the seven days in Genesis 1 were not days of 'creation' but rather days of 'revelation', when God simply showed Adam how he had previously created the world. The week of Genesis 1 was a literal week that occurred around 6000 years ago (making it consistent with biblical genealogies), but it was one of revelation. Creation itself could have occurred over an immeasurably longer period – indeed billions of years.

This is an interesting theory, but the clear suggestion of the biblical text is that the six days of creation refer to days when creation actually occurred. If they were days of 'revelation', why doesn't the text just say so?

1.2.4
What a difference a day makes

A theory that is hugely popular today concerns the nature of the 'days' in the Genesis account. Rather than literal periods of 24 hours, the 'days' of creation are actually much larger periods of time – perhaps millions or even billions of years long – a bit like the use of the word 'day' in 'Day of the Triffids' or 'day of the mobile phone'. Like Chalmers' 'gap theory', this view attempts to 'heal the rift' between the claims of science and the theological statements of Genesis. The problem is that it is difficult to explain why the text of Genesis consistently repeats the phrase 'and there was evening, and there was morning' and then numbers each day. There is nothing to suggest that the six creative days were anything other than real days as we know them.

Wilkinson, himself a doctor of theoretical astrophysics, also points to a discrepancy between the order of creation in Genesis and what is known of the fossil record on earth.

In the Bible, trees were created before marine creatures, but early fossils suggest that the reverse was true.[9] However, by far the biggest discrepancy is that in the Genesis account the earth was created, and there was 'evening and morning' for three days before the sun and the moon were created. To simply re-interpret the 'days' of creation as 'ages' does little to unite the worlds of science and faith.

1.2.5
Literary approach

Among biblical scholars, including evangelicals, by far the most widely accepted interpretation of the Genesis creation account is one that sees no schism between science and theology – but seeks to take both disciplines seriously. The 'literary approach' hinges on a critical question: what kind of literature is Genesis 1-3? Is the entire Bible simply historical narrative reporting events exactly as they happened? It is acknowledged that the Bible contains lots of different forms of literature. History, poetry, prose, parable, prophecy, allegory, dreams and visions are all present in the Scriptures. For example, in the Psalms the Old Testament variously describes God as a rock, a fortress, a shepherd and a warrior, while the New Testament refers to Jesus as a door, a temple, a lion, a shepherd and a lamb.

If there are many different forms of literature represented in the Bible, the proponents of the literary approach question why we are so keen to defend the interpretation of the Genesis creation story as a literal account. In fact, the NIV translation of the Bible lays out the story of the days of creation passage as a hymn or poem. Each creative day starts with the phrase 'And God said' and each ends with 'And there was evening, and there was morning'. It certainly reads more like poetry, or possibly even liturgy, than history. Indeed, many scholars are convinced that Genesis 1 was originally written with a liturgical purpose for use by the Jewish community in public worship.

Furthermore, there is something interesting about the structure of the events over the six days. By laying out the events of the days in two columns, Ernest Lucas shows a pattern in the text.[10]

Though Lucas' structure does not prove that Genesis 1 is not a literal account as described under the seven days theory, it does demonstrate that the chapter was artistically written and balanced in a way that a literal history might not have been.

If the Genesis account was not intended to be a literal record of 'how' God created the world, but rather a poem explaining the 'why' and the 'who' behind it all, it can sit happily side by side with a modern understanding of the science of the opening seconds of the universe.

The earth was shapeless and empty	
Day 1	**Day 4**
The separation of light and darkness	The creation of the lights to rule the day and the night
Day 2	**Day 5**
The separation of the waters to form the sky and the sea	The creation of birds and fish to fill the sky and the sea
Day 3	**Day 6**
The separation of the sea from dry land and the creation of plants	The creation of animals and humans to fill the land and eat the plants
Day 7	
The heavens and the earth were finished and God rested.	

However, those who hold that the biblical account is literal point out that the literary approach can easily get us into trouble. If we say that the creation account does not report the events as they happened, if the first chapters of Genesis are in a sense a figurative account of creation, at what point do we say that the account returns to straightforward narrative? If Adam and Eve were not the first man and woman on earth, what are we to do with the genealogy of Genesis 5 that details the birth line between Adam and Noah?

1.3
Pick your battles

Whichever of the interpretations of the creation account we choose to believe, there is an obvious broader point. The purpose of the Bible is not to be a scientific textbook and when we choose to treat it as such we fail to grasp its real function – to reveal God!

The Bible is not primarily concerned with *how* the world was made, but rather by *whom* the world was made – about 'The Big Plan' rather than the 'The Big Bang'!

'It is fatally easy to overvalue the importance of science and to exaggerate its place in the human experience. Science is of immense value in its proper field – it can explain many things and provide a means of dealing with a great range of technical problems. But answering the profound questions

> In the USA, the battle between those who want creationism taught in schools and those who resist this has more recently focused on the proposal in some states to teach 'intelligent design' (*see panel*). For some this helps point to a plan behind the world, and thus to a creator. For others, intelligent design begs too many questions. What is certain is that the debate will continue to rage!

of life is not the scientist's province. The ultimate meaning and purpose of life and the universe is a matter for the philosopher or theologian.' (David Field and Peter Toon, *Real Questions*)[11]

Indeed, if the Bible had been written as a scientific textbook it would be understood only by those who had a grasp of the complex theories of physics, chemistry and biology, and utterly meaningless to the average person today. The most gifted scholars 200 years ago would not understand many of

What is Intelligent Design?

'Intelligent Design is the science that studies signs of intelligence', writes William Dembski.[12] ID is a movement that looks for scientific and empirical signs that there is a creative mind behind creation, in the same way that if you were to walk into a garden and find it tended, you might reasonably deduce there was a gardener. It has growing support in the United States among some scientists and theologians.

ID asks whether the nature and structure of the universe show objective evidence of being intelligently designed or not.

ID believes design in the biological and biochemical order can be detected and proven.

ID theorists believe that we know enough about some biomolecular systems for it to be unreasonable to continue to appeal only to natural law and chance events as an explanation of their origin.

ID theorists believe that the claims of Darwinian evolution are in conflict with the evidence of biology.

ID is not an explanation based on ignorance (as in the 'god of the gaps' argument), but on knowledge based on scientific evidence.

ID includes people from a wide range of agendas and theologies. It is compatible with, for example, agnosticism, some forms of theistic evolution, and young-earth creationism.

ID focuses on ways of objectively testing design inferences. It does not 'shut down' science.

ID theorists conclude: 'here is real (not apparent) design: we need to learn more about it'.

Reading the Mind of God: interpretation in science and theology, Dr Philip Duce (Apollos, 1998)

its complexities, and even today, as our world and universe still hold so many mysteries, our top academics would still not be able to understand it completely.

However, the Bible has successfully communicated across the centuries to scientists and laymen alike. Why? Because science and theology are different, and complementary disciplines. As Albert Einstein noted 'Science without religion is lame; religion without science is blind.'[13] As such faith and science, if both stay within their mandate, are firm friends. 'We should not expect Christian faith and scientific truth – and that does not mean all the statements made by scientists – to be in conflict with one another.' (Colin Gunton, *The Christian Faith*)[14]

1.4
What is science?

Science is solely concerned with the questions: What? When? How? As defined by *The Concise Oxford Dictionary* its remit is simple in theory if not in practice: 'The intellectual and practical activity encompassing the systematic [empirical] study of the structure and behaviour of the physical and natural world through observation and experiment.'[15]

Scientists are charged with the task of looking at the universe and figuring out. what it is, how it works and when it came into being. It does not, indeed cannot, answer questions of a spiritual nature because they are beyond the physical world as well as within it.

Science, for instance, might be able to analyse Leonardo's *Mona Lisa* and tell us how he painted it. What kind of paints he used, what colours he had on his palette, how he changed it as he went, even which part of the canvas he painted on first – but what it can never explain is why he painted what he painted in the first place. What were the emotions that stirred him to paint, what inspired him to complete his task rather than give up? And science certainly cannot answer the riddle of her curious smile.

David Wilkinson gives an example closer to home.

'If my wife kisses me, then as a good scientist I can say that what caused that was "neck-muscle movements reducing the distance between two pairs of lips, a reciprocal transmission of carbon dioxide and microbes, and a contraction of orbicular muscles". I would be entirely correct in the scientific description of the reason for the kiss. But I would be a very sad human being! There are other issues of meaning and purpose that are to do with the motives for my wife's actions; that is, she is demonstrating her love.'[16]

The word *science* originally simply meant 'knowledge'. What we now know as 'science' should technically be known as 'natural science' based as it is on knowledge we have collected through studying the *physical* world and discovering some of the laws that it follows. But other sciences, or 'knowledges', include philosophy and theology.

1.5
What is theology?

Roger Forster explains that all sciences 'could be called "mankind's product" derived from the data of the universe that God established at creation. Mankind goes to the data of the universe … he observes it, measures it and probes it as far as he can, until he develops a knowledge which explains why things work the way they do.'[17]

But, as time goes by, humankind makes new discoveries, and so, science itself, keeps developing. For example, it finds that the earth is round, and not flat as it previously supposed. Or, that the earth revolves around the sun, rather than the sun around the earth (as was once assumed). Thus, the study of 'natural science' is continually growing and changing as new empirical (touchable, physical) knowledge modifies its theories and deepens our understanding of how things work. This is how all sciences work.

Forster argues that theology, 'the queen of all sciences', develops in a similar way. 'Theology is also a science, but it draws on a much broader body of data than the material world. It comprises mankind's attempts to understand the data of the Scripture, and from it to build a coherent model by which we may grasp the truth about who God is, and how he relates to his creation … with the goal of gaining a deeper and greater understanding of who it is that we are worshipping.'[18]

The study of theology is, therefore, living and developing as we discover more about our world and more about the Bible. But more than that, it's not just a pursuit for academics and professional theologians – it is the activity of every Christian. The real question is not 'do we do theology?' but 'is the theology (literally "knowledge of God") we do good theology or bad theology?' Why is this distinction important? Because as Nigel Wright explains, 'Getting our ways of thinking and believing right (or as right as we can) is part of the process of getting our ways of living and acting right.'[19]

Jim Packer says: 'As it would be cruel to an Amazonian tribesman to fly him to London, put him down without explanation in Trafalgar Square and leave him, as one who knew nothing of English or England, to fend for himself, so we are cruel to ourselves if we try to live in this world without knowing about the God whose world it is and who runs it … Disregard the study of God and you sentence yourself to stumble and blunder through life blindfolded … [with] no understanding of what surrounds you. This way you can waste your life and lose your soul.'[20]

However, a little personal knowledge of God is worth more than a great deal of theoretical knowledge about him. As Paul told the Corinthians, 'knowledge puffs up … the man who thinks he knows something does not yet know as he ought to know'. (1 Cor 8:1–2) To be preoccupied with theological knowledge as an end in itself, to approach Bible study with no higher a motive than a desire to know all the answers 'is the direct route to a state of self-satisfied self-deception.'[21]

As Jim Packer reminds us, we need to be clear what the purpose of good theology is or the danger is that 'if we pursue theological knowledge for its own sake, it is bound to go bad on us. It will make us proud and conceited. The very greatness of the subject matter will intoxicate us, and we shall come to think of ourselves as a cut above other Christians because of our interest in it and grasp of it…'[22]

So, how can we turn our knowledge about God into knowledge of God? First, we need to submit our minds, our intellectual capacity to the Lord, remembering that 'The fear of the LORD is the beginning of wisdom.' (Psa 111:10) Then,

we need to turn each truth that we learn about God into matter for meditation before God, leading to prayer and praise to God. Put bluntly, true knowledge of God should always lead to the worship of God.

Modern theoretical astrophysicists may be able to trace the history of the universe back to a tiny fraction of a second after the Big Bang but this in itself does nothing to reveal why the universe came into being or by whose design it was made. This is why many eminent scientists throughout history also have had a strong belief in God.

'The Big Bang Theory may be true,' Michael Lloyd says. 'I believe it is – but, by itself, it doesn't tell you how to live … For that you need [not just a cosmology, but] a theology … Having a Person at the heart of reality makes morality a matter of right and wrong, not taste and preference.'[23]

The underlying message of the biblical text is unchanged whether the universe was created in six days, six thousand years ago or in a fraction of a second, 13.7 billion years ago. The truth of the biblical creation account is not only that a personal, creator God crafted the universe, but that he created it with a purpose. Ultimately, it doesn't really matter how or when he did so. The question of faith and science is an interesting, even important, one. But in the end it proves to be a grand distraction from the real message of Genesis which is, ultimately, to give us a true knowledge of God.

QUESTION TIME
1. What would you say are the main messages of Genesis Chapter 1?

2. If Genesis Chapter 1 were all that we had of the Bible, what would we be able to discover about:
- God?
- ourselves?
- the world?

3. 'Getting our ways of thinking and believing right (or as right as we can) is part of the process of getting our ways of living and acting right.'[24] Theology is the activity of every Christian so the real question is not whether we 'do theology' but 'is the theology (literally 'knowledge of God') we do good theology or bad theology?'

Can you identify some examples of good theology and some of bad theology? What impact have these had on the world?

2

GOD AS THE ULTIMATE CREATIVE ARTIST

First off – nothing … but God.

Three in one. The Co-Creators, the Divine Collaborators musing, brooding until they
burst with an eternity's creative urge; ideas exploding in one holy splurge.

The cosmos in chaos – no shape, no form, no function. Just darkness. Total.

Until the great Artist calls "lights!" and launches Project Cosmos. As building
blocks – atoms, one ten-millionth of a millimetre wide, crafted to construct a cosmos.

"Let's make stars, masses of stars – think of a number, add a trillion, times it by the number of trees."

A cosmos 140 billion times the size of our galaxy – as far as our telescopes can see!
From stars programmed to self-steer to the micro balance of the biosphere.

"And let's have some fun with the shapes, sizes, colours, textures."

From fine detail to such extraordinary scale; from amoeba to killer whale. From
plants with medicinal properties to an extravagance of animal species. Until.

"Let's make people, like us … but human. Flesh and blood, skin and bone."

Each of us with 13 million miles of DNA inside; each of us located where body, mind and soul collide.

"Like us … but human:"

Let's set their mental screensaver to throw out questions, spark a hunger to
explore; let's hardwire infinity into their hearts, build in a desire to adore.

Let's make them magnets for the beautiful – design their skin with goose bumps
ready to stand to attention whenever they connect with the wonderful.

Let's make them spark into life as they find rhythm and rhyme,
as they move through time from chaos to design.

Let's make them creative – like us… but human.

And God said, "fantastic!"

By Rob Lacey[25]

Teaching Block 2: The Creator God: The Goodness of Creation

2.1
The good Creator

Gerald Coates, the founder of Pioneer, was interviewed on Radio 4 a few years ago. He found himself in debate with a woman who was a leading secular humanist. Eventually the subject turned to the formation of the universe. 'He believes that God created *some*thing out of *no*thing. How absurd can you get?' she said. Gerald replied, 'To create *some*thing out of *no*thing is difficult. But she believes that *no*thing created *some*thing out of *no*thing. That's a lot more difficult.'

The first sentence in the Bible (Gen 1:1) tells us that 'In the beginning God created the heavens and the earth.' This is an incredibly profound theological statement – one short verse that changes our entire view of the universe and our own place in it. It teaches us that:

- God was around before everything we know came into being – before the first atom there was God.
- God created the heavens and the earth – they did not come about by chance but rather through divine design.
- God alone was responsible for creating everything that exists – there were no lesser gods involved. God did the whole thing.

That God is the sole creator of the universe might at first seem a trifling point, but Genesis was written at a specific point in history, in a specific culture by a specific people – Israel. And the heart of its creation narrative becomes clear when it is read against the backdrop of the popular beliefs and practices of Israel's neighbours.

The surrounding nations each had their own account of creation in which a variety of 'deities' or gods were involved. The creation account of Genesis seeks to 'debunk' these popular, but misguided, religious ideas by stating loud and clear it was the one God who created everything – including the various aspects of nature which were deified by other cultures (such as the sun, the moon, the stars, the sea etc). God had no rivals or even helpers in the work of creation, unlike in every other epic about origins.

For instance, why does the Genesis account put the creation of the sun and moon on the fourth day? One reason could be that sun and moon worship was very common in the ancient world. We know that the sages of Babylon kept detailed astrological charts in the belief that human life

Genesis 1 & 2 represent the starting point for Christian theology in defining many of the basic understandings of God in relation to his world.

- The essential goodness of the created order and the act of creation: '*And God saw that it was good.*' (1:10, 12, 21, 25)
- An understanding of the rhythm of day and night – and of life and time: '*Let them serve as signs to mark the seasons and days and years.*' (1:14-19)
- The calling of the animal kingdom to '*be fruitful and multiply.*' (1:22)
- The imago dei: '*Let us make man in our image, in our likeness.*' (1:26)
- The differentiation of male and female: '*male and female he created them.*' (1:27)
- The call of humankind to be stewards of creation. (1:28)
- The necessity of rest and recreation: '*so on the seventh day he rested from all his work.*' (2:3)
- The partnership and equality of male and female. (2:18ff)
- The concept of marriage as a creation ordinance. (2:24)

was, to some extent, controlled by the motion of the moon and planets. Even today it is very common for people from all walks of life to pay a huge amount of attention to their horoscopes. Genesis debunks all this superstition. The 'heavenly bodies' are simply creations of God hung in the sky, and not even named, but just known as big light and little light. They have no power of their own and are neither to be feared nor worshipped.

'The author of Genesis … [is] … subverting the otherwise universal ancient view that some parts of the creation are at least semi-divine. Not only is the light created before the sun and the moon, but those 'heavenly beings', worshipped as divine in ancient cultures … are almost contemptuously relegated to their place under God. The greater and the lesser lights – 'and the stars also', deities relegated to an afterthought – are simply hung up by God as lights.' (Colin Gunton, *The Christian Faith*)[26]

The repeated refrain of the liturgy of Genesis 1 leaves us in no doubt – one God created it all – and it is good. And decisively, the sixth day, on which we, the most problematic inhabitants of the earth were created, ends with an even more emphatic version of the refrain: 'God saw everything that he had made, and it was very good.' (Gen 1:31)

2.2
God's universe

If there is one Creator God we live in a *uni*verse not a *multi*verse. Creation is essentially one. If the universe has more than one source it is not a universe. It is essentially incoherent – no-one is ultimately in control.

'If there are many gods, then reality is fractured and fragmented. That is very clear from the Greek and Roman gods who each had their own sphere of expertise … so that if you were in love with someone, it was to Venus, the goddess of love, that you had to pray. If you wanted to attack your neighbour, it was to Mars, the god of war, that you had to turn. Unfortunately, however, they were in constant conflict with one another, and would use human beings as pawns in their own battles, as a means of getting back at one another … A polytheistic world view [one that believes in many gods] is necessarily going to be an anxiety-ridden world-view, because you never know who is for you and who is against.' (Michael Lloyd, *Café Theology*)[27]

It is a central claim of the Bible that our universe is essentially one – it has one source, one God, and it is his nature that gives it cohesion and consistency. Everything is capable of harmonising and fitting together. It may not always seem that way, but there is still order when all things are properly orientated around their creator.

This is in stark contrast to the stories of Israel's surrounding cultures, which taught that creation represented:

- The outcome of anger and fear, war and destruction, hatred and violence, betrayal and murder.
- The subjugation of females by males amongst the gods.
- The addition of humanity as a mere afterthought, of little value or concern to the gods.

Against this, the Genesis account is a remarkable manifesto of optimism and hope.

2.3
The creation myths

The *Enuma Elish* (commonly known as the Babylonian Creation Story) recounts the struggle between cosmic order and chaos. It is one of many creation stories or 'myths' from various ancient cultures which has now been rediscovered. There are a few direct similarities between the accounts (for example, 'the deep'; the separating of the waters, the placing of the lights in the heavens) which have led some historians to conclude that Genesis is simply a rewriting of the Babylonian story. But, for all the similarities, there is a set of very significant differences as well. The most important of these is that the Babylon myth describes creation out of chaos, while the Genesis account describes creation out of nothing.

The Genesis narrative draws freely on the same metaphors and symbolism, but it does so in order to refute the theology of this pagan myth, and to assert its own distinctive theology or 'knowledge' about the one true God, the Creator of all.

The various gods that appear in the Enuma Elish myth represent different aspects of the physical world. Apsu (the father god) is the god of fresh water and thus male fertility. Tiamat (the mother god), wife of Apsu, is the goddess of the sea and thus chaos and threat. Tiamat gives birth to Anshar and Kishar, gods who represent the boundary between the earth and sky (the horizon). To them is born Anu (the god of sky), who in turn bears Ea. But these 'sons of the gods' make so much commotion and are so ill-behaved that Apsu and Tiamat plot to kill them. However, their plot is discovered and taking revenge Apsu is killed by them. Ea's wife Damkina then gives birth to Marduk (the patron god of the city of Babylon). Meanwhile Tiamat is enraged at the murder of her husband Apsu, and vows revenge. She creates a host of chaos monsters to do battle with him. But Marduk grows strong and, in single combat, smashes her head with a club and dismembers her. He divides her corpse, using half to create the earth and the other half to create the sky.

Thus, the gods are violent, creation itself is an act of violence, the male gods abuse and subjugate the females and humanity is nothing more than an afterthought.

The biblical creation account stands in massive contrast to all this. It is diametrically opposed to it, giving a direct rebuttal, a theological attack on the errors of the creation stories of the surrounding cultures. It tells a different story – a magnificent story. There is only one God, he is good and his creation reflects his character. And in this good universe created by a good God, sin is always an intruder.

'In the light of this historical context it becomes clearer what Genesis 1 is undertaking and accomplishing: a radical and sweeping affirmation of monotheism vis-à-vis polytheism, syncretism and idolatry … On the first day the gods of light and darkness are dismissed. On the second day, the gods of sky and sea. On the third day, earth gods and gods of vegetation. On the fourth day, sun, moon and star gods. The fifth and sixth days take away any associations with divinity from the animal kingdom. And finally human existence, too, is emptied of any intrinsic divinity – while at the same time all human beings, from the greatest to the least, and not just pharaohs, kings and heroes, are granted a divine likeness and mediation.' (Conrad Hyers, *Biblical Literalism*)[28]

us that the 'earth was formless and empty'. And it is out of this formless emptiness that God draws fullness and self-renewing order.

We rely on the regular nature of the physical world. 'Science proceeds on the basis of order in the universe and our ability to discern it … [and] all things are ultimately dependent on God's faithful upholding of the universe moment by moment, for without the Creator they would not exist.' (David Wilkinson)[29] From simple facts like the boiling point of water at sea level being a constant 100 degrees Celsius, to advanced observations about the structure of molecules – the order of our world reveals the order of its Creator.

But it isn't just the scientists who rely on the order of the universe to do their work. For instance, for countless centuries farmers have relied on the knowledge that spring would follow winter and summer would precede autumn. In fact, the whole of human life depends on the order of creation and the maintenance of that order by its Creator.

2.4
A good creation

At each successive stage of the creation process, on each of the six days, God observes the goodness of what he has made. At the end of the sixth day he sees all that he has made and declares it '*very good*' (Gen 1:31). The creation of something very good can only come from someone who is himself very good – a diseased tree will not bear good fruit.

By contrast, elsewhere salvation was understood as an escape from the world of human existence. There was no value or purpose attached to the physical realm. Meaning was to be sought in detachment from the external world, which anyway was less real than the spiritual realm. Creation was flawed, as after the Fall. The religious task is to rescue one's spirit from this 'fallen' world and escape to the spiritual realm. It is clear that this view is flatly contradicted by Genesis, which sees the world as possessing an intrinsic worth and meaningfulness that stems from the rational will of its good and loving Creator.

2.5
An ordered creation

Another hallmark of the biblical account of creation is the pattern that is repeated each day. God speaks and his commands are fulfilled. He names what he has made and observes its goodness. There is evening and there is morning and a new day begins. The picture that this language conjures up is of a careful, thoughtful, ordered creation. God doesn't haphazardly do a bit here and a bit there. With God there are no afterthoughts or mistakes – instead we encounter structure, purpose and order. Genesis 1:2 tells

2.6
A diverse creation

The diversity of life on earth is so vast as to be almost beyond comprehension. The number of different kinds of insects alone defies belief – biologists have identified well over a million and believe that there are countless species yet to be discovered. There are over 300,000 known varieties of beetle, a fact which led biologist J.B.S. Haldane to conclude that 'God has an inordinate fondness for beetles.'[30] Why, one must ask, should it be so? One can only assume that the wealth of life on earth is due to God's extravagance, and that he takes pleasure in many different things, in diversity. He created the squirrel not because there was any real need for a squirrel – although it has its place in our beautifully ordered world – but rather because he liked the idea of squirrels. Looking upon the natural world it is easy to sense God's sheer joy in creation – you can imagine the delight he felt when he came up with the ridiculous idea of giraffes!

Alphonso the Wise, king of Castile and Leon in the thirteenth century, once remarked: 'Had I been present at the creation, I would have given some useful hints for the better ordering of the universe.' It's an interesting notion – what would the world have been like if one of us had been involved in its creation. We might have decided that night and day was a good idea, but would we have arranged the transition from one to the other so beautifully? There is an extravagant generosity to creation that even Alphonso might have struggled to replicate.

QUESTION TIME

1. Where and how do you find it helpful to worship focusing on creation?

2. Psalm 19:1–4 reads 'The heavens declare the glory of God; the skies proclaim the work of his hands. Day after day they pour forth speech; night after night they display knowledge. There is no speech or language where their voice is not heard. Their voice goes out into all the earth, their words to the ends of the world.' Often in the busyness of twenty-first century life we take God's creation for granted. Where, and how, do we see 'the glory of God' in creation around us?

3. Every culture that has ever lived on earth has had places and objects of worship. Why do people worship? What does our society worship?

4. In a society that believes in science why are horoscopes such big business?

DAY TWO — One God: The Creator God

Teaching Block 3: The Creator God: Human Identity

3.1 What does it mean to be human?

What is it that makes a human *human*? The dictionary simply defines a human being as 'a man, woman or child of the species *Homo sapiens*' and *Homo sapiens* as 'the primate species to which modern humans belong.' (*The Concise Oxford Dictionary*)[31]

Psychologists and philosophers have devoted whole careers to the ongoing search for answers. From the great Greek thinkers to a library full of Hollywood blockbusters – *AI, Star Trek, Bruce Almighty, iRobot, Equilibrium* and *The Matrix* to name just a handful. We are fascinated.

There is no escaping the difference between humans and animals. But the question is: What exactly is it?

'A great deal of scientific work has been done in the attempt to work out the difference between human beings and animals. At a purely scientific level the difference is not easy to specify. For example our genetic code differs by less than 2% from that of a chimp. Sensitivity to pain and capacity for intelligent behaviour are often mentioned, but animal studies show these are differences of degree rather than kind. Other differences are claimed, such as:
- The ability to learn, plan and conceptualise
- The use of developed tools, language and counting
- An artistic sense
- The ability to integrate a wide range of knowledge
- The ability to make intuitive acts of judgement
- Moral sense
- The capacity for language and abstract thought brings with it power to reflect on pain and death
- Altruism
- Self-consciousness
- Soul'

(David Wilkinson, *BST The Message of Creation*)[32]

However, the Bible's view of humanity transcends all other ideas of what it is to be human – it is built on one key statement contained in Genesis 1:26–27 that links humans with 'the image of God'.

> Then God said, 'Let us make man in our image, in our likeness, and let them rule over the fish of the sea and the birds of the air, over the livestock, over all the earth, and over all the creatures that move along the ground.'
>
> So God created man in his own image, in the image of God he created him; male and female he created them.
>
> God blessed them and said to them, 'Be fruitful and increase in number; fill the earth and subdue it. Rule over the fish of the sea and the birds of the air and over every living creature that moves on the ground.'
> (Gen 1:26–28)

This claim serves as the foundation for the task of constructing a Christian 'anthropology' or understanding of what it means to be a person. For Christians, the challenge of answering the question 'What does it mean to be human?' is that of grappling with what is known as the *imago Dei*.

3.2
Made in the image of God

Imago Dei is Latin for 'image of God' and has come to be used as the theological term to denote the nature of the relationship between God and humanity. But, not only is it foundational to a Christian view of what it means to be human, more than that, it is essential to understanding a whole range of other key issues such as:

- Human rights and responsibilities
- The sanctity of life
- Stewardship of creation
- Our desire for communication

'[Gen 1:26–28] is the linchpin of the biblical teaching regarding … the *imago Dei* … [but] the text harbours a series of perplexing exegetical obstacles that heighten the difficulty of understanding what the ancient writers sought to communicate by the concept,'[33] says the late Stanley Grenz, until recently Professor of Theology and Ethics at Regent Theological College in Vancouver.

So, what does it mean to be made in God's image? Human beings are stamped with the image of the Creator, called to a personal relationship with him, which defines human life as more than merely biological. When we stand before another person, however destitute, disabled, diseased or degraded, we stand before a '*vehicle of the divine*'. (Howard Peskett & Vinoth Ramachandra, *BST The Message of Mission*)[34]

MIRROR IMAGE

When I became a Christian life wasn't too good, the image of disability in those days was not very positive. Indeed it is fair to say that the norm was out of sight out of mind. I remember most of my education being in 'special' schools most of which were in the middle of nowhere with very little social contact. As I grew up I learned that people either saw people with disabilities as the object of pity or as superheroes battling bravely against the odds. The trouble is that, for me at least, I don't want to be pitied but I don't want to have to be a superhero everyday – I just want to live my life.

In recent years I have become more acutely aware of this dilemma. As a Christian, churchgoer and recently ordained minister I am aware that disability causes intellectual problems for Christians, especially when it comes to miracles and healing. I know that people are perplexed that, having prayed for me, I do not get out of my chair and I am not miraculously cured of my cerebral palsy. Even worse, I want to take part in church activities!

I think we have a problem with image. We tend to look on disability as a tragedy. I have often heard it said I couldn't live the life you do or if I became disabled I would want to die. I understand some of the reasons for this – I remember being in a group discussion in which one person said that every time he looked at me he felt sick. Fortunately he went on to explain what he meant; the image of me being in a wheelchair reminded him of weakness, sickness and all those other negative feelings that we don't want to admit.

In the end as a Christian I can only look to God, and when I read the Bible I see a totally different reaction. First of all I am like everybody else alive or who has lived – made in the image of God. In that respect I am no different. As Paul said in his letter to the Galatians 'there is no difference between slave, free, male or female… we are all one in Christ.'

As for why I haven't been healed, I simply don't know. I also can't explain why Paul wasn't healed when he asked the Lord to take away a particular problem (2 Cor 12:7–9) – but I know it wasn't because of his sin or a lack of faith.

I think we need to start realising that we are all disabled, that's why Jesus came! It is time to realise that when you look at the image of people with disabilities, what you actually see is yourself and Christ.
Alyn Haskey

French biologist Jean Rostan puts it this way: 'For my part I believe there is no life that … does not deserve respect and is not worth defending with zeal and conviction … I would almost measure society's degree of civilization by the amount of effort and vigilance it imposes on itself out of pure respect for life.'[35]

The early church writers believed that God's image consisted of certain attributes, qualities or capabilities that are lodged within the core structure of each and every person. These correspond to qualities in God himself and it is because of their presence that humans can be said to be made in 'the image and likeness of God'. The list of qualities they suggested was long, but two were universally hailed as centrally constituting humans to be 'like God' – those of reason and free will. In the thirteenth century Thomas Aquinas[36] suggested that the divine image is present in all humans as the power to know and love God, which leads to a natural hunger for God.[37] [38]

The *imago Dei* is seen in:

> Our spiritual nature
> Our sense of moral obligation
> Our longing for union with God
> Our aspiration to goodness
> Our desire for community

3.3
The broken image

When the creation week was finished, God considered the world 'very good'. However, it was not long before man's selfishness and greed got the better of him. Genesis 3:1–24 tells the devastation story of the Fall of humankind. But though the Fall is devastating, it is the freedom given to humanity in creation which allows for it to take place. It was only because Adam and Eve were capable of sin (i.e. that they had free will) that they could enter into true relationship with God. Without choice no relationship can ever be real. We have the choice to be in a genuine relationship with God only because we also have the ability not to be. So the Fall is deeply ruinous, but still points to the goodness of creation. The question that confronts us is this – is God's image lost through our sin?

The early Christian writers believed that the *imago Dei* remained present in humankind after the Fall, regardless of whether or not a person chose to acknowledge God. Whatever the *imago Dei* consisted of, it was the essence of what made a person human and therefore could not be lost.

As Augustine taught, 'Although worn out and defaced by

losing the participation of God, yet the image of God still remains.'[39] For him, each and every person, however far they have wandered from God, continues to bear the imprint of God in their life.

However, in the second century Irenaeus introduced the idea that there was a difference between the 'image' of God (which he agreed was to do with reason and will and could not be lost) and the 'likeness' of God (which he saw as true rationality and believed was lost through the Fall and could only be restored by Christ).

This 'two tier' idea was taken up by countless other Christian writers, who over the centuries, though they differed over exactly what the two terms represented, all agreed that whereas the 'image' of God is permanent, or indelible in all people, the 'likeness' of God was somehow lost through the Fall and could only be restored through a relationship with Christ at conversion, through discipleship, or fully and finally in heaven.

Contemporary scholars are now agreed on several main points:

- Contrary to the widely accepted thinking from the early church era through to the Middle Ages, 'selem [image] and demut [likeness] are synonymous or at most offer only a slightly difference in meaning.' (Stanley Grenz)[40] The Hebrew noun selem (image) which appears 17 times all in the Old Testament means 'representation' (Claus Westermann)[41] and demut (likeness) which appears 25 times in the Old Testament means 'resemblance' or 'blueprint', 'model' or 'exact copy'.

- The divine image is not a particular human quality but the fundamental relationship between the humans and their Creator. It is this that makes humankind human rather than just another animal. Claus Westermann says, 'The relationship to God is not something which added to human existence; humans are created in such a way that their very existence is intended to be their relationship to God.'[42]

- There is no scriptural evidence that sin destroys the divine image. The imago Dei remains universally present after the Fall. Stanley Grenz explained that this is shown by the use of the terms for 'likeness-to-God' selem and demut in Genesis 5:1b–2, 3 and 9:6. These

In the ancient Near East (Egypt, Mesopotamia) the idea that an image of a god served as the dwelling place of the spirit of that god was common. A human being could therefore be the dwelling place of a deity.

understand the imago Dei as being passed from Adam to his offspring, although not in quite the same way as described in Genesis 1:26, 27. 'The scholars are agreed … that according to the Old Testament the person's 'likeness-to-God' was not lost with the 'fall', but remained part of humanity'.[43] The image may be blurred, but is not obliterated. Also, there is New

2

CAN YOU SEE THE IMAGE OF GOD IN YOUR CLIENTS?

I am a barrister who defends criminals. My clients are terrorists, murder men, armed robbers, international drug traffickers, city fraudsters, money launderers and the heads of a couple of well known criminal families.

When I started out some 13 years ago, it was smack head shoplifters, street dealers, prostitutes in punch-ups and pub glassings.

From the girl drug addict who has three ways to sustain her habit – thieve, sell drugs or sell herself (for her the image of God is sold for £50 on the Bayswater Road) through to the crime family boss who has created generational wealth and whose sons go to public school, the same questions are always raised.

But ask me, can I see the image of God in them? My heartfelt answer is resoundingly in the affirmative.

The story of one of my 'killer' clients is indicative of nearly all.

His mother was a young black crack addict who raised him in the 90's amidst her own battles – a few days of trying to be a good mum, then back on the game to pay for what went into her veins; the father, a white man, who still lived locally and dealt drugs in a half hearted way refusing to acknowledge the son, even though they lived on the same estate. At 14, the son makes a more formal approach to his father. "F*** off you black bastard" is the paternal response. The killer to be loses his grandmother, the one good influence, who dies in his teens. On a diet of chips and booze he still develops a good height and physique. He is compelling to women and he runs a variety of girlfriends. In his late teens, he determines to be the Big Man locally. For him, that vision entails getting his own car and heaps of bling. He does not have the capacity for greater

vision even as a criminal. He starts to deal, successfully at first with cocaine and cannabis. He still watches his mother and won't do smack. He starts to consume his own product. Then heroin like his mum. Gear makes him unstable and he slaps his main girl. She too is addicted. A child arrives; then another. He has a lot of other crack women but always returns to her. He loves her.

He hears his own bulk dealer further up the chain wants to enforce the debt he owes - a debt he can't pay. He borrows a gun in drink. In a crack rage, he kills the other man. He wakes up in a jail house with a head that only works to hurt and a body panging cold turkey.

After a month of meeting his solicitor, he and I meet for the first time. Can I see the image of God in him? Yes, yes, yes and yes!

continued ➡

Testament evidence that human beings are still seen in the image of God in James 3:9, 'With the tongue we praise our Lord and Father, and with it we curse men, who have been made in God's likeness'.

3.4
The royal image

'A text without a context is a pretext.' In other words, the exploration of the meaning of any verse or passage of the Bible will always be greatly helped by studying the culture of the people to whom it was originally written. What presuppositions, outlooks, beliefs and opinions shaped their understanding of the world?

The fact that Genesis simply uses the term *imago Dei* and then fails to unpack its meaning any further 'assumes that the assertion … did not need to be explained further, because the concept was readily understood by people of that era.' (Werner Schmidt)[44] Genesis (like the rest of the Bible) was not designed as a thesis to be debated by PhD students but a book to bring hope, pastoral comfort and encouragement to ordinary people as they lived out their lives for God in a difficult and testing situation. Whatever its precise meaning, the term 'the image of God' must have made plain and obvious sense to its original audience.

As we have already seen, the Genesis creation narrative is just one of a number of creation stories that circulated around the ancient Near East in the first and second millennium BC. Therefore to understand the meaning of 'the image of God' in Genesis 1 we have to view it as, in some sense, a Hebrew response to their message.

Now, on remand he will be dry and clean. Unaddled by 'class A' drugs for the first time since puberty.

My first yes – is because, whether spoken directly or not, he has deep remorse, not just for himself – and perhaps not for the man that he shot and half buried – but for the mother who never cared for him; for the girls he treated so badly and for the children he may now not see for 25 years. In his pain for these others, the image of God is clear in him. He interrupts our prison conferences to talk about them. They come to him at night.

My second yes – is for the distance between where his life is today and where it could have been if he had sought to live it – or if he had half a chance to live it. Hence, I have found there is a sense that it is often when the biblical promise of life abundant is at its most remote that the image of God is most visible.

And yes again – for the goodness that I found in him as the months of preparation for trial move on. The eyes that change from when we first meet – deepening in a way. The casual discovery from a prison psychiatric assessment report that he is a prison "listener" who is called out of his cell at night to try and talk to other troubled souls in a prison Samaritan capacity; in the decency he shows to me – against a background of being raised amongst folk who would feel no compassion for him.

And yes too – just sometimes – now that he is three years down the track. You hear he attends the Prison Fellowship Alpha course every Saturday, the sixth he has attended! Then you hear too of how he helps lead one of the smaller groups, of how his words like those of Job, are now keeping other men on their feet. Yes, he has terrors to face but he is now a reed that will not be allowed to break.

He may, in Christ, have journeyed further into God's image. A prison Alpha worker who met him recently tells of a man utterly transformed.

He, like all of us, can step into or out of God's image; but only to a degree. In our origins and in its potential for redemption, God's image overarches us all.

Truthfully, it is often easier – very much easier – to see the image of God in my criminal clients than in some of the professionals that I encounter. The vain glory and self obsession that often seems to attach to the city dwelling professional lawyer, and I include myself readily, crusts the soul in a manner which in my estimate makes the image of God sometimes much more difficult to discern than in the killer they might represent.

Stephen M. Ferguson
barrister

2

3.5
God and hierarchy

Into a world laden with oppressive hierarchy, and dictatorship which sees ordinary people as the pawns of the powerful, God speaks.

'Whereas Egyptian writers often spoke of kings as being in God's image, they never referred to other people in this way. It appears that the Old Testament has democratised this old idea. It affirms that not just the king, but every man and woman, bears God's image and is his representative on earth.' (Gordon Wenham, *Genesis*)[49]

The writer of Genesis 1:26 deliberately undermines the popular belief of the time that it was only the monarch who was the divine representative – instead the whole of humankind enjoys that privilege and responsibility. This is nothing short of a revolution. The *imago Dei* is universalised.

Israel's surrounding societies were all hierarchically structured. At the top of the social pyramid was the king, who was believed to represent the local god. Just below him came the priests. Below them came the bureaucrats, the merchants and the military while at the very base of the pyramid came the peasants and slaves. In this way the social order was given religious legitimisation by the creation mythologies of these societies and the poor were oppressed in the name of the local deity.

'The Genesis "counter myth" undermines this widespread royal ideology. It "democratises" the political order. All human beings are called to represent God's kingship through the whole range of human life on earth.' (Howard Peskett & Vinoth Ramachandra, *The Message of Mission*)[50]

And because, here in Genesis, it is not only the kings and powerful lords of the earth who constitute the image of God – but all people everywhere – it follows that the way we treat our fellow human beings is a reflection of our Creator.

In the ancient Near East (Egypt, Mesopotamia) the idea that an image of a god served as the dwelling place of the spirit of that god was common. A human being could therefore be the dwelling place of a deity and, as a result, function as an image of that god. And, of course, the most likely human to fill this important role in any society was the king who was regarded 'as the life-long incarnation of the god.' (D.J.A. Clines)[45] So, for instance, in ancient Egypt the Pharaoh was regarded as 'the image of God living on earth.' (Gerhard von Rad)[46]

Taking this further, in the ancient Near East an image of the king was viewed as the representative of the king. 'Ancient Assyrian kings, for example, erected statues of themselves in conquered territories, probably to represent their occupation of the land.' (Stanley Grenz)[47] In 1979 a statue of an Aramean king (dated around the ninth century BC) was discovered in northern Syria with an inscription where the statue itself is referred to as the 'image' and 'likeness' of the king. According to the inscription King Hadad-Yithi placed this statue of himself in a city to remind his subjects of him and his rule when he was physically absent from them.

And even more, it was generally understood that: 'The image is no mere symbolic portrayal of the king, but stands in a spiritual union with him'. (D.J.A. Clines)[48] There is a sense in which we are supposed to physically represent God. It is in this context, and as a response to it, that the Genesis 1 reference to the *imago Dei* was written.

3.6.
God and the sexes

In most English translations of the Bible, God is referred to in male terms. This is not to say that the Bible presents God as male. There are a few instances where God is described using female imagery (Isa 46:3–4, 49:15; Hos 11:1–4). But the more important truth is that God is presented as a person, as 'he rather than it', not 'he rather than she'. But if oppression on the basis of class is dealt a blow by the Genesis 1 creation account, so is its cousin 'sexism'. It is male and female together who are created in God's image. It was not that having created Adam, God left it at that. Adam on his own could not represent the image of God. But further than that, Eve is taken from Adam's side – not from his head or his feet. The language of the author is deliberate. There is no hierarchy of the sexes in Genesis 1 and 2. 'Observe too that… women are called to share in the dominion of the earth alongside men. This high view of the women was unique among the cultures of the time, and has remained unique well into the modern age.' (Peskett & Ramachandra, *Mission)*[51]

Of course, despite the equality presented in Genesis, Israel was a patriarchal society and projected its elevation of men onto God, thinking that 'God must be male'. However, God is not a man or a woman – God is God. We were made in his image – male and female together – and we should try to avoid the temptation to remake him in ours. That we refer to God in male terms should in no way be used to support the subjugation of women.

3.7
God and individualism

The Genesis account reflects none of the individualism which is such a feature of our Western world today. We make a huge mistake if we assume Genesis 1:26–27 addresses individuals as individuals in the modern sense. Instead 'the divine image characterizes and defines the species as a whole.' (Phyllis Bird, *Male and Female He Created Them)*[52] The Bible never conceives of people in overly-individualistic terms, but always as being interdependent and inherently connected to the rest of society. 'Likeness to God cannot be lived in isolation. It can only be lived in human community.' (Jürgen Moltmann, *God in Creation)*[53] The poet Maya Angelou once wrote; 'While I know myself as a creation of God, I am also obligated to realize and remember that everyone else and everything else are also God's creation.'

The *imago Dei* is related to all men and women, to humankind as a whole, rather than either the king individually or exclusively to the male. God has endowed humankind as a whole with the vocation to act as his partner and representative within creation.

3.8
God and creativity

Part of what it means to be made in the image of God is that we are endowed with freedom, and with the gift and privilege of ongoing creation. Creativity, however we choose to use it, is intrinsic to human life. God did not choose to impose limits on what we can do, even those things that might harm us. Instead, out of his love, he gave us freedom to use, or abuse, the world as we see fit. So, every song written, whether in praise of God or denial of him; every poem; every painting or sculpture; every tool of medicine or weapon of war; every construction of stone and steel or of the mind; every thought, word and deed is an outcome, in the fullest sense, of the great truth that we are made in the image of our Creator. That we have often misapplied this creativity does nothing to undermine our freedom in the image of God. The ongoing act of using and exploring

our God-given creative gifts – of creating order out of chaos, beauty out of formlessness – is God's gift to humanity.

GOD MAKES ME WANT TO SING

The great thing about singing is that it's something anybody can do. We all sing whether we know it or not because it's a God given human instinct to wrap our emotions around a melody and let out what we can't 'talk'. Whether it's 'Abide with me' on the football terraces, 'Silent Night' at the kids' nativity or 'Amazing Grace' on a Sunday morning, God created us to sing and the world is a better place when we do. Singing together is all about 'quantity' not 'quality' as we join our hearts and minds in 'one' song and leave our individualism at the door for a brief moment. It has power when we unite because two is better than one and because 4000 in a big top belting out 'redemption songs' is better than two.

Our songs are not just service 'fillers' but genuine opportunities at changing our towns and cities all over the world. Like when the Israelites sang to celebrate the rebuilding of the walls of Jerusalem it says the sound could be heard 'far and wide' in all the surrounding towns (Neh 12:43). The devil cowers when the saints sing because in these moments we lift our gaze to Jesus the one and only saviour of the world and see our lives as they really are. We begin to have God's heart for the world he created and become people of 'light' whether it's lobbying to see 'poverty made history' or simply slipping a neighbour twenty quid to get some food. We are the army of God, the greatest choir on earth and without your voice it is not complete.

Martin Smith
lead singer with Delirious?

3.9
God and stewardship

'No definition of the image is complete which does not refer to this function of rulership,' D. Clines writes.[54] Genesis is clear, God said: 'Let us make man in our image, in our likeness, and let them *rule over* the fish of the sea and the birds of the air, over the livestock, over all the earth, and over all the creatures that move along the ground' (Gen 1:26) and 'Be fruitful and increase in number; fill the earth and *subdue it*.' (Gen 1:28)

Rulership or dominion over creation is a consequence or outcome of being created in the divine image. Because, according to Genesis, the *whole* of the human race, and not just the king, is in the image of God and because dominion is a royal task, dominion becomes humanity's task. History is littered with examples of those for whom 'dominion' has become licence for 'domination'. There is no thought of that here in Genesis where the word implies responsible stewardship. And if there is any ambiguity then it is cleared up by Genesis 2:15, which states: 'The LORD God took the man and put him in the Garden of Eden to work it and take care of it.' The only other two places where these two verbs 'to work' and 'to take care of' are used is when speaking of service of the priests in the tabernacle (Num 3:7–8; 8:26; 18:5–6). The care of creation is a form of service and worship offered to God. As Ronald Sider puts it, 'Our dominion must be the gentle care of a loving gardener, not the callous exploitation of a self-centred lordling.'[55]

So humankind is given a mandate from God to *subdue* the earth, which means to manage, nurture and enrich it. Not only the earth itself, but all the rest of its creatures are entrusted to human care. You don't have to read any further than Genesis 1 to grasp the extent of our God-given human responsibility in this area.

'Man is placed upon earth in God's image as God's sovereign representative, summoned to maintain and enforce God's claim to dominion over the earth.' (Gerhard von Rad, *Genesis*)[56] With the gifts of creativity and freedom comes the responsibility that necessarily accompanies them. Indeed, we are 'God's vice-regent on earth' (Gordon Wenham,

Genesis) [57] and the fact that it is in such a sorry state reflects nothing but our negligence.

The pollution of air and water supplies, the pillage of nature, the profligate use of fossil fuels, the disappearance of the rainforests, the tragedy of desertification and soil erosion, with the resulting climate changes and the threat to biodiversity – all these which have been characteristics of human societies across the earth – whether due to ignorance, poverty, neglect, civil war, political corruption, commercial greed or personal selfishness. However, the pursuit of economic justice, social peace and a care for creation go hand in hand as outworkings of humankind's responsibility as stewards of God's earth.

The dominion we were given over the earth has all too easily been turned into domination and abuse of it. However, our misuse of the earth and its resources, far from implying a deficiency within the Genesis account, has instead to do with our misunderstanding of what our stewardship of it is supposed to look like.

Understanding the problem is one issue. To repent as individuals, as communities, as nations and as a global family and to begin to search for solutions is another.

'Christians, especially those from rich nations, need to preach and demonstrate a gospel that has the power to liberate men and women from individual and collective idolatries, and to work with all who aspire for a more responsible use of the world's resources.' (Peskett & Ramachandra, *Mission*)[58]

Our God is the Creator God.

QUESTION TIME

1. Bearing in mind what we have explored by 'all human-kind is made in God's image', how does that affect (a) our view of our neighbours (b) evangelistic strategies (c) church mission intentions?

2. In 1994 the World Evangelical Fellowship issued 'An Evangelical Declaration on the Care of Creation'. It states: 'We urge individual Christians and churches to be centres of creation's care and renewal, both delighting in creation as God's gift, and enjoying it as God's provision, in ways which sustain and heal the damaged fabric of the creation which God has entrusted to us.'[59] How can (a) you (b) your family and (c) your church respond to this?

3. If we 'measure society's degree of civilization by the amount of effort and vigilance it imposes on itself out of pure respect for life' (C. Everett Koop)[60] what are our society's three greatest strengths and three greatest weaknesses?

4. Mohandas K. Gandhi said that you must '*Be the change you want to see in the world*'. What changes do you want to see in the world? What changes will you need to make to accomplish them?

5. What does the principle of *imago Dei,* our being made in the image of God, mean for our understanding of:
- Justice?
- The common good?
- Human rights?
- The right to life?
- The sanctity of life?

FURTHER READING

Café Theology by Michael Lloyd (Alpha, 2005) is a brilliant, easy-to-read guide to Christian theology that explores Love, the Universe and Everything.

The Bible Speaks Today: The Message of Creation by David Wilkinson (IVP, 2002) is a practical and accessible study of the theology of creation written by a theologian who is also an astro-physicist.

Old Testament Ethics for the People of God by Chris Wright (IVP, 2004) has an excellent section on ecology and the role of humanity on the earth.

Can we believe Genesis today? by Ernest Lucas (IVP, 2001) helps to explain the literary view of the creation story in particular, and the far-reaching way that scientific truth can interact with the Bible.

1 Kings 18:16–46

Elijah on Mount Carmel

So Obadiah went to meet Ahab and told him, and Ahab went to meet Elijah. When he saw Elijah, he said to him, "Is that you, you troubler of Israel?"

"I have not made trouble for Israel," Elijah replied. "But you and your father's family have. You have abandoned the LORD's commands and have followed the Baals. Now summon the people from all over Israel to meet me on Mount Carmel. And bring the four hundred and fifty prophets of Baal and the four hundred prophets of Asherah, who eat at Jezebel's table."

So Ahab sent word throughout all Israel and assembled the prophets on Mount Carmel. Elijah went before the people and said, "How long will you waver between two opinions? If the LORD is God, follow him; but if Baal is God, follow him."

But the people said nothing.

Then Elijah said to them, "I am the only one of the LORD's prophets left, but Baal has four hundred and fifty prophets. Get two bulls for us. Let them choose one for themselves, and let them cut it into pieces and put it on the wood but not set fire to it. I will prepare the other bull and put it on the wood but not set fire to it. Then you call on the name of your god, and I will call on the name of the LORD. The god who answers by fire—he is God."

Then all the people said, "What you say is good."

Elijah said to the prophets of Baal, "Choose one of the bulls and prepare it first, since there are so many of you. Call on the name of your god, but do not light the fire." So they took the bull given them and prepared it.

Then they called on the name of Baal from morning till noon. "O Baal, answer us!" they shouted. But there was no response; no-one answered. And they danced around the altar they had made.

At noon Elijah began to taunt them. "Shout louder!" he said. "Surely he is a god! Perhaps he is deep in thought, or busy, or travelling. Maybe he is sleeping and must be awakened." So they shouted louder and slashed themselves with swords and spears, as was their custom, until their blood flowed. Midday passed, and they continued their frantic prophesying until the time for the evening sacrifice. But there was no response, no-one answered, no-one paid attention.

Then Elijah said to all the people, "Come here to me." They came to him, and he repaired the altar of the LORD, which was in ruins. Elijah took twelve stones, one for each of the tribes descended from Jacob, to whom the word of the LORD had come, saying, "Your name shall be Israel." With the stones he built an altar in the name of the LORD, and he dug a trench round it large enough to hold two seahs of seed. He arranged the wood, cut the bull into pieces and laid it on the wood. Then he said to them, "Fill four large jars with water and pour it on the offering and on the wood."

"Do it again," he said, and they did it again.

"Do it a third time," he ordered, and they did it the third time. The water ran down around the altar and even filled the trench.

At the time of sacrifice, the prophet Elijah stepped forward and prayed: "O LORD, God of Abraham, Isaac and Israel, let it be known today that you are God in Israel and that I am your servant and have done all these things at your command. Answer me, O Lord, answer me, so these people will know that you, O Lord, are God, and that you are turning their hearts back again."

Then the fire of the Lord fell and burned up the sacrifice, the wood, the stones and the soil, and also licked up the water in the trench.

When all the people saw this, they fell prostrate and cried, "The Lord—he is God! The Lord—he is God!"

Then Elijah commanded them, "Seize the prophets of Baal. Don't let anyone get away!" They seized them, and Elijah had them brought down to the Kishon Valley and slaughtered there.

And Elijah said to Ahab, "Go, eat and drink, for there is the sound of a heavy rain." So Ahab went off to eat and drink, but Elijah climbed to the top of Carmel, bent down to the ground and put his face between his knees.

"Go and look towards the sea," he told his servant. And he went up and looked.

"There is nothing there," he said.

Seven times Elijah said, "Go back."

The seventh time the servant reported, "A cloud as small as a man's hand is rising from the sea."

So Elijah said, "Go and tell Ahab, 'Hitch up your chariot and go down before the rain stops you.'"

Meanwhile, the sky grew black with clouds, the wind rose, a heavy rain came on and Ahab rode off to Jezreel. The power of the Lord came upon Elijah and, tucking his cloak into his belt, he ran ahead of Ahab all the way to Jezreel.

The BIG ISSUE

Teaching Block 1

The Universal God: **The God of the Whole Earth**

Teaching Block 2

The Universal God: **A Multi-Faith World**

Teaching Block 3

The Universal God: **The Task of the Church**

The BIG ISSUE

On Monday 10 June 2002 the Queen chose to celebrate the diversity of the UK's different faiths by inviting 800 guests from what the BCC referred to as 'Britain's nine historic faiths – the Baha'i, Buddhist, Christian, Hindu, Jain, Jewish, Muslim, Sikh and Zoroastrian traditions' – to a reception 'as a signal of [her] respect for all religions in Britain, not just the Church of England, of which she is head.'[61]

We live in a multi-cultural, multi-ethnic, multi-linguistic, multi-ideological, multi-faith society. Our major cities are vibrant, cultural melting pots. Mayor Ken Livingstone has referred to London – where more than 300 languages are spoken – as 'the world in a city'. It is a kaleidoscope of thinking, traditions and tastes. Most major and many minor religions are increasingly present in towns and cities across the UK.

We are bombarded by voices with different messages. 'Life will be all the richer for learning to live in harmony,' we are told. Others go further: 'All religions are equally valid, diverse, cultural understandings of God.' But equally there are those who fear our lives and communities are under threat as we are swamped by beliefs and customs from other cultures and faiths. And, at the same time, we are only too well aware of the dangers of religious fundamentalism. Indeed, we are attacked for it ourselves.

'All religions are prone to [fundamentalism] given the right circumstances,' Polly Toynbee claims. 'How could those who preach the absolute revealed truth of every word of a primitive book not be prone to insanity? There have been sects of killer Christians and indeed the whole of Christendom has been at times bent on wiping out heathens.'[62]

Religious pluralism affects our children and grandchildren even more profoundly than it does us. It is here to stay, and demands a practical response from us as individuals and churches. So we must ask ourselves:

- Is our God the God of the whole world or just our private world?
- Is the Bible's revelation of God unique or just one view among many?
- Is Christian truth 'objective truth' or only 'true' for those who choose it to be so?
- How should we respond to the new multi-cultural, globalised world on our doorstep?

Teaching Block 1: The Universal God: The God of the Whole Earth

1.1 The Old Testament

1.1.1 The God of Israel

One of the most significant prayers in the Jewish faith is the *Shema* – 'Hear, O Israel, the Lord our God, the Lord is one.' (Deut 6:4) For literally thousands of years that simple prayer has been on the lips of generation after generation of Jews – from Moses to David, from Jesus to Jonathan Sacks.

Faithful Jews, around the world, pray the *Shema* at least twice a day. It is the first prayer they learn as infants and is, for many, the last they utter before death.

The *Shema* may seem a simple text, but it contains a depth of theology. Its chief task is to affirm the identity of God. The one and only true God is Yahweh, and Yahweh is not only without equal, he is without competition. He is not part of a system of 'gods' like those that captivated the surrounding nations – the god of the river, the god of the field, the god of the mountain, the god of fertility, the god of the sun and so forth. Instead, he is the sole Creator of all that exists.

'The Shema … is a call for the loyalty of the people …

One God: The Universal God

[it] has direct and concrete implications. It is a call for the Israelites to live their lives under the Lordship of one God and not under the tyranny of the many gods … Judaism loudly proclaims that there is only one God and he is Lord of every aspect of life … Polytheists can compartmentalise life and distribute it among many powers … Monotheists … have only one reference point…. The implications are far reaching, not as simple theology, but as practical missiology. (Michael Frost & Alan Hirsh, *The Shaping of Things to Come*)[63]

The *Shema* also affirms the covenant. It is the daily articulation, the proclamation of who God is and whose people the Israelites are. This reminder and reinforcement of the truth offered Israel the reassurance they needed for daily life. Its words delivered security and assurance. In a world that was thought to be in the hands of territorial, competitive and often warring deities whose power and influence was only ever limited and local, the words of the *Shema* rang out like a

The Shema

שְׁמַע | יִשְׂרָאֵל, יְיָ | אֱלֹהֵינוּ, יְיָ | אֶחָד

Sh'ma Yisrael Adonai Elohaynu Adonai Echad.
Hear, Israel, the Lord is our God, the Lord is One.

בָּרוּךְ שֵׁם כְּבוֹד מַלְכוּתוֹ לְעוֹלָם וָעֶד.

Barukh Shem k'vod malkhuto l'olam va-ed
Blessed be the Name of His glorious kingdom for ever and ever.

וְאָהַבְתָּ אֵת יְיָ | אֱלֹהֶיךָ, בְּכָל-לְבָבְךָ, וּבְכָל-נַפְשְׁךָ, וּבְכָל-מְאֹדֶךָ.

V-ahavta et Adonai Elohecha b-chol l'vavcha u-v-chol naf'sh'cha u-v-chol m'odecha.
And you shall love the Lord your God with all your heart and with all your soul and with all your might.

וְהָיוּ הַדְּבָרִים הָאֵלֶּה, אֲשֶׁר | אָנֹכִי מְצַוְּךָ הַיּוֹם, עַל-לְבָבֶךָ:

V-hayu ha-d'varim ha-ayleh asher anochi m'tzav'cha ha-yom al l'vavecha.
And these words that I command you today shall be in your heart.

וְשִׁנַּנְתָּם לְבָנֶיךָ, וְדִבַּרְתָּ בָּם

בְּשִׁבְתְּךָ בְּבֵיתֶךָ, וּבְלֶכְתְּךָ בַדֶּרֶךְ וּבְשָׁכְבְּךָ,

V-shinantam l-vanecha, v-dibarta bam
b-shivt'cha b-vaytecha, u-v-lecht'cha ba-derech u-v-shachb'cha u-v-kumecha.
And you shall teach them diligently to your children, and you shall speak of them when you sit at home, and when you walk along the way, and when you lie down and when you rise up.

וּבְקוּמֶךָ. וּקְשַׁרְתָּם לְאוֹת | עַל-יָדֶךָ, וְהָיוּ לְטֹטָפֹת בֵּין | עֵינֶיךָ,

U-k'shartam l'ot al yadecha, v-hayu l-totafot bayn aynecha.
And you shall bind them as a sign on your hand, and they shall be for frontlets between your eyes.

וּכְתַבְתָּם | עַל מְזֻזֹת בֵּיתֶךָ וּבִשְׁעָרֶיךָ:

U-chtavtam al m'zuzot baytecha u-vi-sharecha.
And you shall write them on the doorposts of your house and on your gates.

From Deuteronomy 6:4–9

Technically the complete Shema is composed of three Old Testament passages linked together: Deuteronomy 6:4–9 (the core Hebrew prayer), Deuteronomy 11:13–21 and Numbers 15:37–41

charter of hope and liberation. They provided Israel with her 'Big Story' or what we would now call a 'metanarrative'.

'Yahweh is frequently depicted as wanting the sole attention of his people and seeing the worship of any God as infidelity.' (Ruth Jenkins)[64] Even though Yahweh issued the command that he would be Israel's only God, the struggle with other gods and their priests and priestesses continued not only in the early desert years but even later, long after Exodus, when the Jews were settled in the land of Israel. The Old Testament often mentions these other gods – Asherah, Baal, Anath, El, Dagon, and many others – whose temples existed side by side with the worship of Yahweh. So, for the people of Israel the *Shema* was far from a daily lesson in theoretical academic theology – it was intensely pastoral and practical.

1.1.2
The God of the Big Story

A metanarrative is a grand, overarching, all-encompassing account providing a framework which seeks to bring

> The metanarrative or 'Big Story' of the Bible is the story of creation, fall, redemption in history and new creation. If it is the Big Story of the Bible and of Israel, it is also the Big Story of the world.

universal (or 'absolute') truth, order and meaning to life. The term is best known for its use by Jean-François Lyotard, the post-structuralist French philosopher, who wrote, 'I define postmodern as incredulity towards metanarratives.'[65]

Our postmodern culture is characterised by an increasingly widespread scepticism towards these 'big stories' by which former generations lived. It sees them as instruments of control and claims that such overarching systems of belief, whether based on science, a political ideology or a religion 'have always served the interests of the winners in the historical process and enabled them to retain their hold on power and privilege.' (David Smith, *Mission After Christendom*)[66]

Writer and art critic John Berger writes. 'Never again will a single story be told as though it is the only one.'[67] In our globalised, postmodern society, metanarratives (which are

The Shema – the central prayer in the Jewish prayerbook

It is its opening line that makes the Shema so significant: 'Hear O Israel, the Lord is our God, the Lord is one'. For Jews, it is a declaration of faith, and also an assertion that God is one and indivisible. So much of Judaism is concerned with observing practical laws – both positive and negative, both ethical and ritual – that the Shema stands out as a cry of belief, something that cannot be simply carried out or avoided but has to be personally taken to heart.

The Shema has also acquired special symbolism because of historical circumstances. After Rome had conquered the land of Israel, there was one last attempt at freedom: the Bar Kochba revolt in 135. It failed, and one of the leading rabbis who had supported it, Akiba, was tortured to death in the arena. He died saying that first line of the Shema as a final act of spiritual defiance. Ever since then it is traditional for a Jew who is about to pass away to recite the Shema as his/her final words.

However, the rest of the prayer/passage is also important, being a checklist of how to put beliefs into practice and give

them concrete form. First, there is the general advice that love of God should permeate one's being ('all your heart … soul … and might'). Then there is the quintessentially Jewish notion that to be a good Jew it is not enough to believe and practise oneself, but one has to pass it on to the next generation and keep the faith going. Hence the command to 'repeat these words to your children'. It goes on to emphasise that Judaism is not just for once a week on the Sabbath, nor reserved for a special place of worship, but for all times of the day and week, and in every place ('when you sit in your home and walk in the street, when you lie down and rise up'). It also adds two particular rituals as reminders: wearing special prayer boxes (phylacteries) at midweek morning services, inside which is the Shema. Similarly one should mark the front door of one's house with a small container or 'mezuzah', which also has the Shema in it, and acts as a daily reminder to the occupants to adhere to Jewish values and traditions.

Rabbi Dr Jonathan Romain MBE
Maidenhead Synagogue

3

But if Yahweh is Israel's one God he is also the *world's* one true God. As the people of Israel prayed the *Shema* they were doing more than inviting the tribal gods of the surrounding nations to move along the shelf a little to make room for Yahweh among their number. They were being ordered to vacate the shelf altogether. Yahweh alone is the true and living God – the God of the whole earth. (Psa 24:1)

Right from the start, with the account of the creation, the covenant with Noah (Gen 6), the choosing of Abraham for the benefit of 'all peoples on earth' (Gen 12), the covenant with David (1 Sam 16) and onwards, we encounter through the Bible a God who not only claims to be lord of all, but has laid out a plan for all of his world and its peoples. The Old Testament relentlessly announces Yahweh's *universality*.

As God's people – and God *was* God of Israel in a unique way – Israel was required to maintain a distinctiveness from

now forced into much greater direct competition with one another – for example, Christianity and Islam) have lost much of their ability to convince. According to Lyotard and many other post-structuralists and deconstructionists there is no big story – no absolute truth. Truth is what I decide it to be. Indeed, it is argued, any attempts to construct a grand theory about life and meaning dismiss the naturally existing chaos and disorder of the universe.

Yahweh – The distinctive, personal name of the God of Israel

Moses said to God, "Suppose I go to the Israelites and say to them, 'The God of your fathers has sent me to you', and they ask me, 'What is his name?' Then what shall I tell them?"

God said to Moses, "I AM WHO I AM. This is what you are to say to the Israelites: I AM has sent me to you." (Exod 3:13, 14)

The Hebrew for God's name, the name that he gives Moses to describe what he is really like, who he really is, is YHWH. It is sometimes translated Jehovah in older English translations of the Bible.

YHWH is the most frequently used name for God in the Old Testament. It appears over 5,000 times. It is known as the *Tetragrammaton* (Greek: word with four letters).

YHWH was written with four consonants only. Ancient Hebrew had no written vowels – or even vowel points. These were added much later, by which time pronouncing the name of God had already been forbidden for generations. One of the theories is that Jewish people stopped saying the 'name' out of fear of violating the third commandment, 'You shall not take the name of YHWH your God in vain' (Exod 20:7, literal translation). Still today,

when the term is read out loud by Jews it is universally substituted with the word *Adonai*, *Elohim*, *Hashem* or *Elokim*, depending on circumstances.

According to Rabbinic tradition, YHWH continued to be pronounced by the high priest on Yom Kippur (the Day of Atonement), the only day when the Holy of Holies of the Temple would be entered. However, with the destruction of the Second Temple in the year AD 70, this use also vanished and the original pronunciation was totally lost.

It is significant that God deliberately chose to be known by a personal name, and not a title, but this is lost by the way it is translated in English. 'We should get used to thinking of YHWH as the personal name for the LORD when we read it in the Old Testament,' writes Chris Wright. Yahweh is used wherever the Bible stresses the personal character of God and his direct relationship with those human beings who have a special relationship with him.

According to one Jewish tradition, YHWH means 'to be, to become'. Another regards it as meaning 'He was; He is; He will be'. Other interpretations include 'I am the one who is' and 'I AM. the one I AM.' Many scholars believe that the most proper meaning may be 'He brings into existence whatever exists'.

the nations around, to keep themselves holy for the Lord. This was a moral and spiritual difference, but not a matter of social prejudice, hatred or alienation. In fact, they were commanded to love the alien.

Tragically, however, Israel misunderstood the privilege they enjoyed as the 'people of God'. They saw themselves in an exclusive relationship with little or no responsibility towards the peoples of the world. The stubbornness of Jonah and his reluctance to preach to the people of Nineveh is a graphic symbol of this tragic attitude. Israel regarded Yahweh as their own local and tribal god – the god of the Israelites – and if you weren't one of them you couldn't get to know him.

1.1.3
The one true God

George Bernard Shaw famously quipped, 'God created man in his image – unfortunately man has returned the

---

In his book *Christianity Rediscovered*, Vincent Donovan writes about his time living and working among the Masai in Tanzania, East Africa. He tells of how they told him of their god Engai, who loved rich people more than poor people and healthy people more than the sick. Engai loved good people because they were good, but hated evil people – 'those dark, evil ones out there' – and punished them for their wickedness. In fact, Engai loved the Masai more than all the other tribes; and he loved them fiercely, jealously and exclusively. His power was known throughout the lush grasslands of the Masai steppes; his protection saved them from all the surrounding, hostile, Masai-hating tribes. He assured them of victory in war and his goodness could be seen in the water and rain, the cattle and children with which he provided them.

Donovan, an Irish-American missionary, says that these stories reminded him of those about Israel, which he knew so well from the Old Testament. Perhaps here was his best opportunity to talk to the Masai about his God, the God of Israel. So he finally spoke up and told them they reminded him of another great people.

'They are the Hebrew tribe, the Jews, the Israelis. They are famous the world over for having preserved the knowledge of the one, true God. But it was not always easy for them. They often tried to restrict that God to their tribe and to their land and so made him less of a God than he really was … The God of the tribe of Abraham had become a God who was no longer free. He was trapped in that land, among that tribe. He had to be freed from that nation, that tribe and that land, in order to become the High God.'

Donovan says that he realised that at this point he had touched a sensitive nerve with the Masai. He continued, 'Everyone knows how devout you Masai are … you have known God and he has loved you. But I wonder if you have not become like the people of the tribe of Abraham. Perhaps God has become trapped in this Masai country, among this tribe. Perhaps God is no longer free here … Perhaps you Masai must also leave your nation and your tribe and your land, at least in your thoughts, and go in search of the High God, the God of all tribes, the God of the world … Free your God to become the High God. He is the God not only of the Masai, but … of every tribe and nation in the world … The God who loves rich people and hates poor people? The God who loves good people and hates evil people? The God who loves us because we are good and hates us because we are evil? There is no God like that. There is only one God who loves us no matter how good or how evil we are.'

After Donovan had finished speaking there was a long, thoughtful silence. Perhaps he had gone too far. What would their response be? Eventually an elder spoke, 'This story of Abraham – does it speak only to the Masai? Or does it speak also to you? Has your tribe found the High God? Have you known him?'

Donovan opened his mouth to give his assured answer. But no words came out. Instead, through his mind raced thoughts of religious division and hatred in Ireland and the certainty with which Americans believe that 'almighty God' will always bless their side in war; images of the God who loves good people, industrious people, clean people, rich people and punishes bad people, lazy people, dirty people, thieving people, people without jobs and on welfare. Which god is that, he thought.

'No we have not found the High God,' Donovan finally answered ashamedly. 'My tribe has not known him. For us, too, he is the unknown God. But we are searching for him… Let us search for him together. Maybe, together we will find him.'[68]

3

1.2
The New Testament

Jesus lived and worked in a world characterised by religious and cultural plurality and his response to it was startling. Whenever he encountered people from outside the Jewish community he confronted them with the claims of the true God, but always without condemnation. At times, they showed extraordinary insight into the identity of Jesus, and he recognised and commended their faith. They may have had a distorted view of God, but that was never where Jesus chose to begin.

favour.' His comment echoed the work of his contemporary Emile Durkheim, one of the founding fathers of sociology, who suggested that humans worship the gods that they create. Each tribe invents a god that reflects its values, standards, aspirations, hopes, ambitions and attitudes. Then they worship it – and so legitimise and endorse their own behaviour. For instance, many of Israel's surrounding nations worshipped pagan fertility gods. These gods then conveniently demanded that the men engage in sexual intercourse with religious or 'cultic' prostitutes! (They argued that this was intended to encourage the deities, by imitation, to be fertile in their land.) Durkheim's work is a powerful argument and offers important warnings to us all. The trappings of our twenty-first century pagan culture too easily entice us – and when they do inevitably our image of God becomes distorted. But more than that, as Archbishop William Temple pointed out, 'The more distorted a man's idea of God and the more passionately he is committed to it, the more damage he will do.'

> **Jesus' attitude towards Gentiles was considerably more inclusive than that of the Jewish establishment.**

'When Jesus had entered Capernaum, a centurion came to him, asking for help. "Lord," he said, "my servant lies at home paralysed and in terrible suffering." Jesus said to him, "I will go and heal him." The centurion replied, "Lord, I do not deserve to have you come under my roof. But just say the word, and my servant will be healed. … When Jesus heard this, he was astonished and said to those following him, "I tell you the truth, I have not found anyone in Israel with such great faith. I say to you that many will come from the east and the west, and will take their places at the feast with Abraham, Isaac and Jacob in the kingdom of heaven. But the subjects of the kingdom will be thrown outside, into the darkness, where there will be weeping and gnashing of teeth."' (Matt 8:5–12)

This would have posed an enormous challenge to Jewish exclusivity – Jesus dares to teach that some Gentiles (people of non-Jewish origin) will be involved in the 'big feast' of the kingdom of heaven. This alone was enough to brand him dangerously heretical, but he goes on. There are others, he says, who think they belong – whose religious credentials are impeccable – but who will be thrown out. Then, to add insult to injury, he announces that the centurion's faith was greater by far than any he had observed in Israel. It is clear that

Jesus' attitude towards Gentiles – those formally engaged in the 'wrong' religion – was considerably more inclusive than that of the Jewish establishment.

Jesus' endorsement of the faith of the centurion, together with the fact that his condemnation fell squarely and consistently on the *leaders* within the Jewish community, should have given his followers a clue. It was not so much the traditions of Judaism that mattered, but faith in Jesus himself.

But it was to take a while longer for that penny to drop.

1.2.1
Seeds of hope

Jesus' followers were again confronted with the universality of the gospel, through some of his parables. In the parable of the wedding banquet (Matt 22:1–14) the first, restricted invitation to the feast is undoubtedly a reference to the election of Israel. But the parable goes on to depict the abuse of that privilege and the subsequent throwing open of the invitation to everyone. In the parable of the sheep and the goats (Matt 25:31–34) Jesus stresses the universality of his ministry as he refers to the last judgment when all the nations will be gathered. When we read this, it appears at first glance that Jesus makes his separation on the grounds of good works, whereas within the overall scheme of scripture we know that people are saved by the grace of God and faith in Christ alone. (Eph 2:4–5)

This passage challenges our neat formulas of conversion and reminds us that authentic discipleship must result in good works and great fruitfulness. James 2:14–26 reminds us that 'faith without works is dead'.

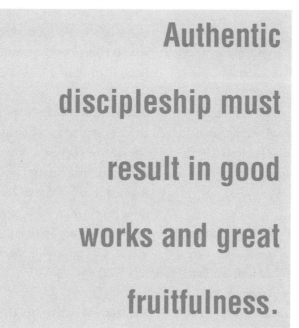

Authentic discipleship must result in good works and great fruitfulness.

The parable is also more than provocative where Jesus and Israel are concerned. 'If you are really the people of God,' Jesus seems to declare, 'then your light will shine before the nations and the poor and the dispossessed will receive the good news due to them.' For those of us heeding Jesus' words in the here and now, the parable challenges our own understanding of God's activity in human history while reminding us that history itself is ultimately his story.

1.2.2
The early church

The first Christians lived in an environment where the air was filled with the conflicting truth claims of other religions and it was under this intense pressure that their own beliefs were honed and strengthened. However, in its first years the early church was an extremely Jewish institution – Gentiles were not often welcomed. The great significance of the incarnation in opening up salvation to the whole world was temporarily lost on the first Jewish believers in spite of the fact of Jesus' repeated words (Matt 28, Acts 1, etc.) about the universalising of the influence of the gospel. As far as the Jews were concerned Jesus had come to set *them* free – his life, death and resurrection was a fulfilment of ancient promises made to *their* people.

It is because of the church's early exclusive attitude that circumcision was later to become such a big debate in Acts and Paul's letters. The question was a simple one: 'If someone wants to become a Christian, do they first have to become a Jew?' Though the answer seems obvious to our modern minds, in the first century it was far from straightforward. Christianity may be a new thing, but it was still part of the 'big story', and that story was fundamentally about Israel. What they had to understand was that God's intention for Israel had always been that the blessings of the covenant would not be confined to ethnic Israelites (Jews), but would be opened up to include people of all nations – as God had promised Abraham. The meaning and identity of Israel had been expanded through Christ.

1.2.3
A paradigm shift

Acts 10 was a turning point, a paradigm shift. As the story unfolds we learn that Cornelius, a centurion in the Italian Regiment, is visited by an angel. The angel tells him that God has seen his good deeds and heard his prayers. He is then instructed to send some men to Joppa to bring back Peter, Jesus' disciple, to stay with him.

At the same time Peter saw a vision of a sheet being lowered from heaven that contained all kinds of animals that were considered 'unclean' under Jewish law. God instructs Peter to abandon his old ways and no longer to view any food as being unclean: 'Do not call anything impure that God has made clean.' (Acts 10:15) He is then told to go downstairs, meet the men sent by Cornelius and to go with them.

When he arrived at Cornelius' house, Peter made a startling speech:

'You are well aware that it is against our law for a Jew to associate with a Gentile or visit him. But God has shown me that I should not call any man impure or unclean. So when I was sent for, I came without raising any objection … I now realise how true it is that God does not show favouritism but accepts men from every nation who fear him and do what is right.' (Acts 10:28–29, 34–35)

As Peter spoke the Holy Spirit fell on everyone listening and they started 'speaking in tongues and praising God.' The Jewish believers who had accompanied Peter were astonished that these people – unclean Gentiles – had received the Holy Spirit. 'Then Peter said, "Can anyone keep these people from being baptised with water? They have received the Holy Spirit just as we have." So he ordered that they be baptised in the name of Jesus Christ.' (Acts 10:47–48)

Suddenly everything had changed. The salvation available through Jesus was clearly available to the whole world, not just the Jews. And though there would still be lots of questions on the finer points of how all this was to be worked out, the radical message of God's inclusivity was starting to sink in.

QUESTION TIME

1. Why did the Jews turn the 'one God of the whole earth' into their tribal god?

In what ways have we turned God into our tribal god? How is our image of God distorted by our culture?

2. George Bernard Shaw famously quipped 'God created man in his image – unfortunately man has returned the favour.' What do you think Shaw was referring to?

3. While addressing a centurion Jesus said these words: 'I tell you the truth, I have not found anyone in Israel with such great faith. I say to you that many will come from the east and the west, and will take their places at the feast with Abraham, Isaac and Jacob in the kingdom of heaven. But the subjects of the kingdom will be thrown outside, into the darkness, where there will be weeping and gnashing of teeth.' (Matt 8:10–13) Do Jesus' words have any implications for our local churches? If so, what?

3

Teaching Block 2: The Universal God: A Multi-faith World

2.1 Three important definitions

In thinking about how Christianity relates to the other world faiths, the church has used three different terms to describe three different approaches – exclusivity, inclusivity and pluralism. There is however, unfortunately, no consensus throughout the church on the precise meaning attached to these words. The following definitions are suggested by Harold Netland in his book *Dissonant Voices*[69] and have been widely used. Indeed, Netland himself acknowledges that these are simply working definitions and may be too rigid for some.

Exclusivism (or *particularism*) maintains that the central claims of Christianity are true, and that where the claims of Christianity conflict with those of other religions, the latter are to be rejected as false. Christian exclusivists also characteristically hold that God has revealed himself definitively in the Bible and that Jesus Christ is the unique incarnation of God, the only Lord and Saviour. Salvation is not to be found in the structures of other religious traditions.

Inclusivism, like exclusivism, maintains that the central claims of the Christian faith are true, but it adopts a much more positive view of other religions than does exclusivism. Although inclusivists hold that God has revealed himself definitively in Jesus Christ and that Jesus is central to God's provision of salvation for humankind, they are willing to allow that God's salvation is available through non-Christian religions. Jesus is still held to be, in some sense, unique, normative, and definitive, but God is said to be revealing himself and providing salvation through other religious traditions as well. It is the attempt to strike the delicate balance between the affirmation of God's unique revelation and salvation in Jesus Christ and openness to God's saving activity in other religions that distinguishes inclusivism.

Pluralism parts company with both exclusivism and inclusivism by rejecting the premise that God has revealed himself in any unique or definitive sense in Jesus Christ. To the contrary, God is said to be actively revealing himself in all religious traditions. Nor is there anything unique or normative about the person of Jesus. He is simply one of many great religious leaders who have been used by God to provide salvation for humankind. Pluralism, then, goes beyond inclusivism in rejecting the idea that there is anything superior, normative or definitive about Christianity. Christian faith is merely one of many equally legitimate human responses to the same divine reality.

2.2 Faith and culture

For many centuries, European churches, both Protestant and Roman Catholic, viewed themselves 'as champions of the Christian faith' and 'saw it as their duty to spread not only their civilization around the world, but also their faith. The two were often seen as being intertwined.'[70]

However, one unfortunate result of this 'intertwining' was that Western colonial Christianity often demonstrated a naïve and negative attitude both to other religions and cultures. Though there were wonderful exceptions, to a large extent many missionaries ignored the need to relate the Christian message to the beliefs of other religions, firmly believing that there was no connection between the two – simply a radical discontinuity.

In 1792 William Carey, the father of the modern missionary movement, wrote: 'Can we as men, or as Christians, hear that a great part of our fellow-creatures … are enveloped in ignorance and barbarism? Can we hear that they are without the gospel, without government, without laws, and without arts, and sciences; and not exert ourselves to introduce amongst them the sentiments of men, and of Christians? Would not the spread of the gospel be the most effectual means of their civilisation? Would not that make

> **People around the globe are more connected to each other than ever before.**

them useful members of society? … even … those who at present seem to be scarcely human?'[71]

As farsighted as Carey was in many other ways, his emphasis on the link between Christianity, human advancement and Western civilisation is clear and provides a window into the attitudes and thought patterns of his day. Indeed, at the height of European colonial power Hilaire Belloc could make the provocative claim that 'the faith is Europe and Europe is the faith.'[72] European culture was seen as normative and ultimate – an attitude which tended to foster both an air of superiority and, it has to be admitted, arrogance towards all other non-European cultures and religions. The richness of their heritage often went unnoticed, while their deficiencies were ruthlessly exposed.

2.3
Culture wars

However, as in previous eras, it proved impossible to contain the message of Christ within a single culture and over the course of the twentieth century this was to become ever clearer. Fast and safe travel, first by sea and later by air, meant that for the first time it was possible to travel between countries and continents quickly and cheaply. People living thousands of miles away were no longer distant, unknowable groups but instead became neighbours only a few hours' travel away.

Easy travel also led to huge levels of economic migration. People began moving in great numbers over thousands of miles to seek out a better life. The streets of the seats of colonial power were seen to be places of great riches. Thus, England in the 1950s witnessed the arrival of large

---

William Carey was born in 1761. A shoemaker, converted at 18, he became a preacher among the Strict Baptists. During the 1780s, God gave him a great burden for those who had not heard about Christ, and in 1792 he founded what is now the Baptist Missionary Society. He wrote *An Enquiry into the Obligations of Christians* to use as means for the conversion of the heathens, which argued the missionary case as:

- a logical and practical assertion of the obligation resting upon all Christians
- a commission from God still binding on us
- a task requiring piety, prudence, courage and forebearance
- a task needing fervent and united prayer

"Surely it is worthwhile to lay ourselves out with all our might, in promoting the cause and kingdom of Christ?"

One God: The Universal God

parish in Southall is 36% Sikh, 21% Hindu, 20% Muslim, and only 16% Christian (2001 census data). London is now described as the most cosmopolitan place on earth – 300 languages; 30% of its residents born outside the UK; and every major world faith represented.

Suddenly, the absolute attitudes of Christianity found themselves being challenged by similar 'absolutes' from other religions. It became increasingly difficult to believe that the rest of the world's citizens were 'savages' as our imperial past had suggested.

Now, at the beginning of the twenty-first century, people around the globe are more connected to each other than ever before. Information and money flow more freely than ever. Goods and services produced in one part of the world are increasingly available in all parts of the world. International travel is more frequent. Global communication is commonplace. Events in one part of the world have immediate implications for us all. We know this phenomenon as 'globalisation' and it increasingly describes the political, economic, cultural and religious environment in which we all live.

immigrant populations from Asia, the Caribbean and Africa with a consequence that foreign cultures were no longer 'over there', but instead 'over here' – indeed, even on the same streets. The religious ramifications of this migration have been huge. Societies that had previously been, if not monolithically Christian, at least structured in such a way that Christianity was seen as being the default with minority faiths largely pushed out of sight in terms of public policy and discourse had to begin to rethink.

> **Is salvation available to humankind other than that provided for us by God through Christ?**

'For the Christian churches in Britain, no longer were other faiths a distant reality located in far-off lands. British Christians found during the second half of the twentieth century that their neighbourhoods had come to include growing numbers of adherents of non-Christian religions. These new faith communities brought the symbols of their faiths with them, so British towns that had previously been home only to Christian places of worship found increasingly that their skylines were shaped by Muslim mosques, Hindu temples, Sikh gurdwaras and so forth. This process stimulated the churches to reassess their attitudes towards these faiths.' (Peter Riddell, *Christians and Muslims*)

In North West London, for example, one Church of England

'Young European Christians on holiday in Egypt, or Indonesia or India come face to face with 'people' who belong to other religious traditions and make the disturbing discovery that they do not necessarily fit the stereotypes of the 'unreached peoples' they have heard about endlessly in Evangelical churches back home. Such travellers are likely to return asking what the term 'unreached' actually means in relation to people who have demonstrated qualities of integrity, hospitality and spirituality that are noticeable by their absence in Western societies … meanwhile, older and more experienced Western Christians … now routinely encounter Muslims and Hindus as colleagues and neighbours and suddenly find themselves wrestling with precisely the [same] kind of issues.' (David Smith, *Mission After Christendom*)

2.4.
The universe of faiths

If life in our globalised, multicultural, post-Christendom world has created a new awareness of other faiths and cultures, it has also served to highlight some old, but foundational and related, questions the church has grappled with since its very inception:

- Is Jesus the only way to God – the universal saviour or simply one of a number of alternatives?
- Is there any truth in other religions?
- How should we respond to other faiths and treat members of them?
- On what basis will members of other faiths be judged?
- Is salvation available to humankind other than that provided for us by God through Christ?
- Is God's grace available to everyone regardless of their religious or social background or is it dependent on the evangelistic obedience or otherwise of the church?
- Can a person who did not know him in their earthly lifetime be saved by Christ?
- If the most devout Christians had been raised in an Islamic context would they not, very likely, be devout Muslims? Is salvation based on a kind of geographical lottery?
- If a person lives outside of the influence of Christianity are they outside the scope of salvation?
- What about those people who have never had the

opportunity to hear the gospel? Are they condemned for eternity through no fault of their own?

- Is the God of love really content to consign the vast majority of the population of earth to hell? (Although not all Christians would be happy with phrasing the question in that way.) Would God, a God of universal love, ordain that only the Christian minority of the human race can be saved?

These are huge questions which, as Christians, we can't avoid.

2.5
The third way

After having come into contact with Hindus, Sikhs, Muslims and Jews in the 1950s and 1960s, John Hick, a Presbyterian theologian, recognised that many of these people were ardent believers in their respective faiths and that their morality, ethics and behaviour were in many aspects similar to those of the average Christian. Attempting to respond to this he began to talk about what he called the 'universe of faiths'. Where traditional Christian thought had placed Christianity as the 'sun' in the system, around which the other faiths would orbit, Hick put God.

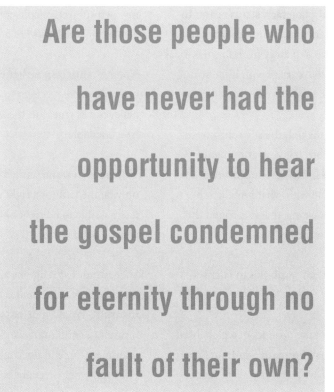

Are those people who have never had the opportunity to hear the gospel condemned for eternity through no fault of their own?

'The Copernican revolution in astronomy consisted in a transformation of the way in which men understood the universe and their own location within it,' Hick wrote. 'It involved a radical shift from the dogma that the earth is the centre of the revolving universe to the realization that the sun is the centre, with all planets, including our own earth, moving around it. And the Copernican revolution in

theology must involve an equally radical transformation … It must involve a shift from the dogma that Christianity is at the centre to the thought that it is [God] which is at the centre and that all the religions of mankind, including our own, serve and revolve around him.'[73]

Hick was propounding what we now describe as a 'pluralist' approach.

But this simple move has serious implications. If Christianity ceases to be the centre of the system, even if awarded some kind of special 'planetary' status nearer to God, it is still just another planet on a par with other religions. Clearly this is a massive step away from the historical position held by the church, and carries with it the strong assumption that each religion holds its own power to save.

In fact, later, concerned that the polytheistic religions (eg Hinduism) and secular religions (eg secular humanism) were excluded from his model, Hick produced a revised version where he replaced God with what he called the 'absolute' or the 'real'. He now claims that it is round this ultimate truth that all religions circle.

There are a number of important responses to Hick's pluralistic approach.

Pluralism is not new. It is not the product of a globalised world. For instance, the Roman Emperor Septimus Severus hedged his religious bets by having in his private chapel not only the statues of deified emperors, but those of the miracle worker Apollonius of Tyana, Abraham, Orpheus and Jesus Christ. A century ago, Mahatma Gandhi claimed, 'The soul of religion is one, but it is encased in a multitude of forms.' And the Hindu mystic Ramakrishna used to speak

of himself as the same soul that had been born previously as Rama, Krishna, Buddah and Jesus.

Pluralism is logically weak. Ironically, while claiming to be committed to 'relativism' pluralists make a huge number of 'absolute' claims, which in the end are peddled on nothing more than the basis of their own subjective presuppositions. Eventually, a commitment to this kind of relativism leads to a commitment to nothing in particular. Humans, both as individuals and collectively, need to be anchored in some firm foundation in order to find meaning and purpose in the otherwise meaningless flux of relativity. In contrast, a genuinely Christian worldview draws its authority from Jesus Christ, a person about whom there are records which are available for examination.

'Jesus, as I read the New Testament, confronts me as a real person whose words and deeds pose radical questions to me and to my own ideals. There is an objective reality which calls into question my own beliefs, ideals and practices … The Hickian revolution is exactly the opposite of the Copernican. It is a move from a view centered in the objective reality of man Jesus Christ, to a view centered in my own subjective conception of ultimate reality. (Lesslie Newbigin, *The Gospel in a Pluralistic Society*)[74]

Not all 'truth' can be 'true truth'. Logically, any religion can only make its claim to offer salvation because it believes it is true. But these 'truth claims' are often mutually irreconcilable.

'If there is in some sense a real world … then salvation can only be the fruit of a right relation to that real world. And it is possible to be right or wrong in our understanding of what kind of a world it is.' (Ken Gnanakan)[75]

Suggesting that religions are all equally valid surrenders that which is at the centre of them all – a concern to know the truth. Would it be possible for a God of truth to reveal himself in conflicting ways? For instance, can God be an inanimate force in one and a personal being in another? How can what is venerated in one religion be reconciled to the same being anathema in another? How can the God of the whole earth in one religion be one god among many in another? The divine in Hinduism is impersonal, though approached through countless deities and statues. The Muslim Allah is personal, with no subordinate deities and an absolute prohibition of idols. Buddhism is a religion with no God at all. Judaism denies that Jesus was the Messiah. Islam denies that he was the Son of God. Islam denies that Allah ever reveals himself in person to humankind: he reveals only his will. Christianity declares that God reveals his will through his person. Christianity teaches that God forgives. In Buddhism and Hinduism there is no forgiveness, only ruthless *karma* (cause and effect, paying off your guilt), which is the opposite of *grace* (free forgiveness). The goal of all existence in Buddhism is *Nirvana*, meaning extinction or 'complete cessation of both desire and personality' – and was attained by the Buddha after no less than 547 births. The goal of all existence in Christianity is to live once, know God and enjoy him forever. To separate the quest for salvation from the business of understanding what is the truth is a recipe for disaster.

'True truth' can exist. The statement that there is no absolute truth is an assertion for which no proof is offered or can be offered. Though it has become one of the axioms of contemporary Western culture, it is pure unsupported dogma. In fact, it is logically indefensible by its own criteria, i.e. 'There is no true truth except this one!' There is nothing in the nature of things and nothing in the necessities of human thought that requires us to deny the possibility that history might have a centre point just as the solar system has a centre.

We cannot live without 'true truth'. If there is no publicly accepted belief about what human life is for, about its purpose, there is no way in which human conduct can be described as good or bad. Conduct becomes a matter

In July 1989, the Second International Congress on World Evangelisation (Lausanne II) in Manila, the Philippines, produced *The Manila Manifesto*. It stated: '… Because men and women are made in God's image and see in the creation traces of its Creator, the religions which have arisen do sometimes contain elements of truth and beauty…. In the past we have sometimes been guilty of adopting towards adherents of other faiths attitudes of ignorance, arrogance, disrespect and even hostility. We repent of this. We nevertheless are determined to bear a positive and uncompromising witness to the uniqueness of our Lord, in his life, death and resurrection, in all aspects of our evangelistic work including inter-faith dialogue.' [78]

of purely personal choice based on personally preferred 'values'. There are no barriers to halt the gradual slide into moral anarchy which liberal societies are witnessing at the present time.

Pluralism is just another religion. Rather than a synthesis of truth from other religions, pluralism overrides and disregards the distinctives of each of them as it chooses – thus more honestly it should acknowledge itself as yet another religion.

2.6
All truth is God's truth

Though a pluralist approach cannot be squared with the Bible, the question remains about whether there is any truth in other religions.

If God is present in the whole world, his grace (an intrinsic part of his character) too must be at work everywhere, in every country, among all peoples, in all cultures and possibly even within their religious structures. Religions, after all, are humankind's vehicles for finding God, however we conceive him. Ken Gnanakan, an Indian church leader, puts it this way:

'If at all there is a reality called religion, it is because human beings made in the image of God are necessarily God directed. Their attempts to reach God cannot [therefore] be looked at as rebellion, for rebellion is the attempt to go away from God. Separated from God, humankind suffering from alienation seeks to return to its maker, and hence expresses itself in religion.' [76]

To acknowledge that all truth, wherever it is found, is God's truth does not suggest equality between the world religions – it is simply to recognise that a rejection of equality does not imply a denial of commonness. As we've seen, the Christian tradition has always affirmed that there is some provisional knowledge of God in all humankind – all are made in the *imago Dei*. For instance, why did Jesus commend the faith of the Gentiles if that faith did not matter at all? It's not clear how and why some of the Gentiles who responded to Jesus did so. What is clear is that the incoherent faith from their background became faith in Jesus himself. And why did Paul build from, rather than ignore,

to this kind of understanding, 'most times such a stand is not so much biblical as much as traditional, doctrinal or denominational' which he adds 'could be as dangerous as the response of the pluralists.'[77] To build either spiritual ghettos in which to live in isolation from one another, or to follow the path of aggression towards other faiths, with a view to dominating them, are both destructive, self-defeating and clearly non-Christlike responses.

The question that this kind of approach poses is not whether God's revelation through Christianity is complete or not, but rather whether there are any signs of God's partial or 'provisional' revelation in other religions.

the worship of the 'unknown God' when he dealt with the people in Athens in Acts 17?

Ken Gnanakan claims that though some react negatively

Karl Rahner coined the phrase 'anonymous Christian'. Concerned with preserving the uniqueness of Jesus for salvation, he stated that Christ is the norm that brings about salvation wherever people are being saved in all religions,

Christians and Hindus: What common ground do we have?

Hindus are people
It's important to remember this obvious truth, because 'Hinduism' is a very broad term for a religion with many strands, developed over long periods. It is more like 'a tree that has grown gradually', with many branches of culture, philosophy, belief and spirituality. Each Hindu you meet will have their own understanding of what their religion means. It is a way of life, not just a system of belief. There are over 500,000 Hindus in the UK and around 750 million worldwide (the third largest religious community). Hindu philosophies and spiritual disciplines have become extremely influential for millions more.

Hindus believe in God
Most Hindus believe strongly that God is One, the Ultimate Reality and Energy behind the universe. Many also believe that God is manifested in countless ways, including images. Hindus pray every day to know God and to experience truth and peace. Many also attend the local temple, which has increasingly become the focus of community life in the UK.

Hindus want to live good lives
They want to fulfil their duty (dharma), following the guidelines of scripture and tradition, playing their part in

their community. They want to overcome selfishness, pride and bad habits.

Hindus face the relentless pressures of secularism and materialism
Like others from every religious background, some Hindus find their religion irrelevant under this pressure, while others find it more important. Christians have a lot of common ground with Hindus. For example:
- maintaining moral standards
- education of our young people
- celebrating diversity and fighting discrimination
- working for harmony and better understanding between religious communities
- striving for equality of opportunity for people of all ethnic backgrounds.

But, as Christians, our number one priority must be to build bridges of friendship, trust and understanding with Hindus, as well as people of other faiths and cultures, through finding common concerns (like those above) and by working at personal relationships.

Ram Gidoomal CBE
Founder of South Asian Concern

even if his name is not acknowledged. Perhaps the most famous presentation of this view is by Raymond Panikkar.

In his book *The Unknown Christ of Hinduism*, Panikkar speaks of the 'hidden Christ of Hinduism.' He says, 'Hidden and unknown indeed! Yet present there … The good and bona fide Hindu is saved by Christ and not by Hinduism, but it is through the sacraments of Hinduism, through the message of morality and the good life, through the Mysterion that comes down from him through Hinduism, that Christ saved the Hindu normally … Whatever God does *ad extra* happens through Christ.'[79]

However, many others have critiqued Rahner's work as falling into the trap of imperialism. How would we react, they ask, to being called 'anonymous Muslims' (on the grounds that only Allah is God, so whoever thinks they are worshipping God must actually be worshipping Allah)? As Peter Cotterell puts it, 'The honorary granting of Christian citizenship to those who have not asked for it, and who have, in some cases, positively resisted it (as is true of both Muslims and Jews), savours of sheer imperialism.'[80] God's saving work is dependent on his grace, his mercy and his judgement mediated through Christ's achievements.

2.7
Satan and deception

However, in all this the reality of Satan and the Fall cannot be ignored. Religion is not merely about human good intentions, it can also become a demonic deviation away from God. If humankind needs God and seeks to fulfill this desire through religion, Satan also finds in religion an avenue of control and hence diverts the seeker into deception. This is evidenced in terrorist attack on the World Trade Centre of 2001 or the London bombings of 2005. However, we must also remember that Christianity itself is no exception to this rule – consider the way in which the Third Reich were able to co-opt Christianity into the service of racism and militaristic nationalism.

This dark side of religion cannot be ignored or ever edited out of the picture, but neither should we allow it to become the whole picture. The insularity of so much Western Christianity has meant that it has often failed to do justice to the humility, devotion and longing for fellowship with

God that is present in some other religions. Take, for instance, one Muslim prayer from a compilation published by Constance Padwick, who spent years travelling in Islamic countries and amassed an extraordinary collection of devotional material:

'Oh God, some sought from Thee this world and Thou gavest it to them. And others sought from Thee the next world and Thou didst satisfy them. But I ask Thee neither for this world nor for the next, but only for the increase of love in my heart.'[81]

Thus Clark Pinnock, who describes himself as a 'cautious inclusivist' (although many other Christians who would not call themselves inclusivists would find themselves in agreement with him), reminds us that his stance 'does not glorify religions, as though there were not depths of darkness, deception and bondage in them. It avoids being rosy-eyed about religions that can be wicked as well as noble … [it] stops short of stating that the religions themselves as such are vehicles for salvation … [but it] holds that grace operates outside the church and may be encountered in the context of other religions.'[82]

2.8
The ultimate question

The Bible is clear that there is no salvation available to humankind other than that provided for us by God through Christ. Jesus' own exclusive claim leaves us beyond any doubt: 'I am the way and the truth and the life. No-one comes to the Father except through me.' (John 14:6) Therefore, it is clear that whoever will be there in the new creation will be there solely because of the work of Christ, and not on any other grounds.

But having established this truth, an important question still remains. Will sincere, devout and dedicated men and women be saved despite their lack of any observable commitment to Jesus Christ? Does a person need to know about Jesus, hear and respond to an evangelistic presentation of the New Testament gospel before God will save them? Will some of those who did not know Christ in their earthly lifetime be saved by him? Does God have favourites or arbitrarily exclude whole people groups from the possibility of salvation?

One God in a Multifaith Society

One of the greatest challenges to Christianity today is how we are going to relate to Islam. A response simply of fear is always negative. It inevitably leads us to respond by withdrawal (and therefore isolation) or with aggression.

The vast majority of Muslims are not evil militants, but people who have a huge respect for other people of real faith. Most Muslims I meet want to know that I am a good and orthodox Christian. What they have a problem with is Western liberalism that has no respect for the Almighty. What we as Christians need to do is form real relationships with the Muslims we meet showing that we are as serious about our faith as they are about theirs, then and only then do we have a hope for future relationships between us and the Islamic world. It is possible to talk to and work with Islam. Indeed, such dialogue will demand of us that we take new risks – but in doing so our faith will be strengthened not weakened.

Canon Andrew White
President of the Foundation for
Reconciliation in the Middle East

'Nothing could be more remote from the whole thrust of Jesus' teaching than the idea that we are in a position to know in advance the final judgment of God … the last day will be a day of surprises, of reversals, of astonishment. In his most developed parable of the last judgment, the parable of the sheep and the goats, both the saved and the unsaved

Saving Grace and Common Grace

The grace that brings people to salvation is often called God's saving grace.

God also gives people all kinds of blessings that are not part of salvation. This is often called common grace. God has compassion on all people, and goodness is found in the whole of creation. The earth produces not only thorns and thistles, but food and materials for clothing and shelter. People are able to grasp truth and distinguish it from error, and so through that to do good. This is all due to God's common grace.

For he makes his sun rise on the evil and the good, and sends rain on the righteous and on the unrighteous. (Matt 5:44–45)

The LORD is good to all; he has compassion on all he has made … The eyes of all look to you, and you give them their food at the proper time. You open your hand and satisfy the desires of every living thing. (Psa 145:9, 15–16)

These are not different categories of God's grace, but simply different aspects of God's goodness to us.

are astonished. Surely theologians at least should know that the judge on the last day is God and no one else,' Lesslie Newbigin states.[83]

Since God alone knows the heart of every person, how can we judge whether or not another person truly has that faith which is acceptable to him? So it is that Jim Packer concludes:

'We may safely say: (i) if any good pagan reached the point of throwing himself on his Maker's mercy for pardon, it was grace that brought him there: (ii) God will surely save anyone he brings thus far: (iii) anyone thus saved would learn in the next world that he was saved through Christ.'[84]

John Stott explains: 'When somebody asked Jesus, "Lord, are only a few people going to be saved?" he refused to answer and instead urged them to enter through the narrow door (Luke 13:23–24). The fact is that God, alongside the most solemn warnings about our responsibility to respond to the gospel, has not revealed how he will deal with those who have never heard it. We have to leave them in the hands of the God of infinite mercy and justice, who manifested these qualities most fully in the cross. Abraham's question, "Will not the Judge of all the earth do right?" (Gen 18:25) is our confidence too.' [85]

This approach affirms that:

Grace is available universally

Christians have classically made the distinction between 'saving grace' and 'common grace' – the understanding that something of God's revelation, image and creativity is alive in each human person and in the world.

God's blessing, grace and salvation is freely available to all peoples, in all cultures. The grace of God saves us but the universality of this grace is not for us to restrict. As we have seen, it is this very point that Jesus makes in his parables. The grace of God is unreachably beyond our comprehension, let alone our attempts to press it into predictable patterns.

The journey of faith has continuity

Becoming a Christian is not necessarily seen as a radical discontinuity with other religious experience. Martin Goldsmith, an experienced missionary in Indonesia, explains.

'I see exact parallels with much of the church's evangelistic preaching in the area of Indonesia where I worked. People there too believed in 'Dibata' who made the world. Christians then taught about his character as revealed in the Bible and supremely in the person of Jesus Christ. There is always some continuity between other faiths and Christianity.' (Martin Goldsmith, *What about other Faiths?*)[86]

'Every missionary knows that it is impossible to communicate the gospel without acknowledging in practice that there is some continuity between the gospel and the experience of the hearer outside the Christian church. One cannot preach the gospel without using the word "God." If one is talking to a person of a non-Christian religion, one is bound to use one of the words in her language which is used to denote God. But the content of that word has been formed by her experience outside the church. By using the word, the preacher is taking the non-Christian experience of the hearer as the starting point. Without this there is no

way of communicating.' (Lesslie Newbigin, *The Gospel in a Pluralistic Society*)[87]

In the first three chapters of Romans, Paul explains why the whole of humanity needs the gospel, because of our rebellion against God and our idolatry of the created order. But in the middle of his argument, he asserts that there is a knowledge of God available to all humankind. 'For since the creation of the world God's invisible qualities – his eternal power and divine nature – have been clearly seen, being understood from what has been made, so that men are without excuse.' (Rom 1:20) He emphasises that the power and the deity of God is clear to all.

And although ultimately we all need God's grace to respond to him at all, for many this revelation of God leads them to a sincere, though often misguided, quest for ultimate truth.

2.9
Beyond labels

In his book *Christians and Muslims*, Peter Riddell summarises the six key positional statements of what he regards as a biblical approach to other faiths:

- Other faiths may contain elements of truth and beauty.
- Christians may learn something from people of other faiths.
- Christians should allow themselves to be challenged by other faiths.
- Other faiths are worthy of Christian affection, respect, and even admiration in certain ways.
- Other faiths do not represent alternative gospels.
- The biblical witness to God and Christ is complete in itself.[88]

Lesslie Newbigin creatively summarised his own position to the multifaith issue in this way:

'The position which I have outlined is exclusivist in the sense that it affirms the unique truth of the revelation in Jesus Christ but is not exclusivist in the sense of denying the possibility of the salvation of the non-Christian. It is inclusivist in the sense that it refuses to limit the saving grace of God to the members of the Christian church, but it rejects the inclusivism which regards the non-Christian religions as vehicles of salvation. It is pluralist in the sense of acknowledging the gracious work of God in the lives of all human beings, but it rejects the pluralism which denies the uniqueness and decisiveness of what God has done in Jesus Christ.' [89]

2.10
Religions or people

There is, however, one last, but even more fundamental, question to consider. Does God meet men and women on the grounds of their religion or as individuals and even as communities who are prepared to meet him? With the pressure of pluralism we can easily ignore the fact that eventually God is interested in people as people and not merely as Hindus, or Muslims or even atheists. In fact, there is very little justification for claiming that God is transforming religions and secular movements – he transforms people. Our task therefore is to meet people rather than to confront religions. Understanding this as a starting point will help us approach our pluralist society from a totally different perspective. Whether or not there is a continuity or discontinuity between Christianity and other religions, there is always continuity with an individual's journey of faith.

QUESTION TIME

1. In Acts 17:22 Paul said to the Athenians, 'I see that in every way you are very religious.' Paul had definitely observed several things which brought him to this conclusion, chief among them being the altar to 'the unknown God'.

Does Paul see this as a good or bad thing?

Is the continuity that Paul establishes merely a preacher's ploy or more than that?

What lessons are there for our situation today?

2. In her 2004 Christmas speech Queen Elizabeth II said,

'Religion and culture are much in the news these days, usually as sources of difference and conflict, rather than for bringing people together. For me, as a Christian, one of the most important of these teachings is contained in the parable of the Good Samaritan, when Jesus answers the question, Who is my neighbour? … Everyone is our neighbour, no matter what race, creed or colour. Some people feel that their own beliefs are being threatened. Some are unhappy about unfamiliar cultures. They all need to be reassured that there is so much to be gained by reaching out to others; that diversity is indeed a strength and not a threat.'

What do you feel is to be gained by reaching out to others?

Do you feel your own beliefs are being threatened?

How should Christians respond when a mosque is to be built in their neighbourhood?

3 Teaching Block 3: The Universal God: The Task of the Church

3.1 Towards tomorrow

The real problem for Christian mission in the West is not that there is an absence of spiritual hunger within our pluralistic, globalised society, but rather the church's struggle to engage with this longing on the part of so many. Even where such recognition does occur there is often an unwillingness or perhaps an inability to respond in any terms other than those dictated by our existing traditions and structures. But this challenge is not new – we face the same kind of paradigm shifting decisions that confronted the Apostle Peter as he considered what non-Jewish, Gentile Christianity might look like in the first century.

Peter had to learn the difficult lesson that faithfulness to scripture does not necessarily mean 'doing things the way that we have always done them'. Instead, biblical faithfulness calls for a humble recognition that the Holy Spirit may still have more to teach us than we have, so far, been able to receive. Ironically, it is only by way of this kind of thoroughgoing re-imagining of what it means to be the church in our new environment that we will remain firmly rooted in the historic tradition of our faith.

3.2 Our faith is public not private

The uniqueness of Jesus Christ cannot be a claim purely for the Christian community. If the truth about God as revealed in the Bible and chiefly through Christ is true at all it must be true universally – it is either the Big Story for everyone or no story for anyone! Without universal validity Jesus Christ has no resemblance to the One that the New Testament claims him to be. Lesslie Newbigin put it succinctly thus: 'Believing the Christian faith means believing that it is true and is therefore public truth, truth for all, truth which all people ought to accept because it is true.' [90]

Rather than retreating into its own privatised world in order to accommodate other voices, the church's task is to recover the confidence that the gospel is not only a metanarrative but *the* metanarrative or Big Story. In order to do this we must also reject the limited vision of the church as a place of private withdrawal from society. Our faith may be personal but it can never be private.

Recognition of this fact means that we cannot live as though there is one god for the church, another for politics, another for economic life and still another for the home. As the *Shema* teaches, all of life, every aspect of it, is to be brought under and unified under our one God. It is the task of the church to obliterate the deeply unbiblical schism between the sacred and secular so fundamental to old modes of thinking.

'Christians ought not to hope for a society controlled by bishops or church synods … It is through the presence and activity of committed and competent Christian men and women in the various areas of the common life of society that the Christian vision for society could become effective in practice.' [91]

How do we turn these statements into actual practice?

3.3 Our method is dialogue not diatribe

Even though Paul was provoked by the religious idolatry in Athens (Acts 17), he demonstrated a clear respect for the Athenian people. Luke uses two key words to describe Paul's approach to proclaiming the truth about Christ while at the same time respecting the individual right of each Athenian to choose his own pathway. But note that Paul doesn't pull his punches when asked to speak before the city council – he speaks of ignorance, repentance and judgement (Acts 17:30–31).

3

- Acts 17:17 contains the first key word that, in fact, describes the whole of Paul's ministry. 'So he [Paul] reasoned in the synagogue with the Jews and the God-fearing Greeks, as well as in the market-place day by day with those who happened to be there.' The word 'reasoned' is a translation of the Greek word *dialegomai*. It carries the idea of 'discussion'. In fact, it is from this that we get our English word 'dialogue'. Luke also uses it to describe Paul's approach in Acts 17:2, 17; 18:4, 19; 19:9; 20:7, 9. So it seems that when Paul preached he created lots of space for discussion. He gave his audience plenty of opportunity to ask questions, raise disagreements and put their own points of view.

- The second key word *suneballon* (dispute) also carries the idea of discussion. 'A group of Epicurean and Stoic philosophers began to dispute with him.' (Acts 17:18) In other versions of the New Testament this word has been translated 'argue' and 'debate'. This is not one-way traffic – Paul listens as much as he talks and so builds relationship. Once again, it is clear that Paul left lots of room for feedback from his hearers and was not offended by a robust response from them. Honest and open dialogue is the key to Paul's whole approach and effectiveness.

'What is unique about the Christian gospel is that those who are called to be its witnesses are committed to the public affirmation that it is true – true for all peoples at all times – and are at the same time forbidden to use coercion to enforce it. They are therefore required to be tolerant of denial, [but] not in the agnostic sense in which the word 'toleration' is often used … The toleration which a Christian is required to exercise is not something which he must exercise in spite of his or her belief that the gospel is true, but precisely because of this belief.' (Newbigin)[92]

Evangelism and Culture

The development of strategies for world evangelization calls for imaginative pioneering methods. Under God, the result will be the rise of churches deeply rooted in Christ and closely related to their culture. Culture must always be tested and judged by Scripture. Because man is God's creature, some of his culture is rich in beauty and goodness. Because he is fallen, all of it is tainted with sin and some of it is demonic. The gospel does not presuppose the superiority of any culture to another, but evaluates all cultures according to its own criteria of truth and righteousness, and insists on moral absolutes in every culture. Missions have all too frequently exported with the gospel an alien culture and churches have sometimes been in bondage to culture rather than to Scripture. Christ's evangelists must humbly seek to empty themselves of all but their personal authenticity in order to become the servants of others, and churches must seek to transform and enrich culture, all for the glory of God.

The Lausanne Covenant: Clause 10

We use the term 'tolerance' a great deal in our culture. However, we do so in a much diluted form. A dictionary definition is 'the quality of accepting other people's rights to their own opinions, beliefs and actions.' To tolerate is to treat someone with generosity. However, these definitions do not imply agreement. In fact, the only people who can be truly tolerant are those who are confident in what they believe but secure enough to leave space for others to choose their own way.

'We do not seek to impose our Christian beliefs upon others, but this is not because (as in the liberal view) we recognise that they may be right and we may be wrong. It is because the Christian faith itself, centred in the message of the incarnation, cross and resurrection, forbids the use of any kind of coercive pressure upon others to conform.' (Newbigin)[93]

Thus Paul's prayer should be ours too.

'And pray for us … that God may open a door for our message, so that we may proclaim the mystery of Christ, for which I am in chains. Pray that I may proclaim it clearly, as I should. Be wise in the way you act toward outsiders; make the most of every opportunity. Let your conversation be always full of grace, seasoned with salt, so that you may know how to answer everyone.' (Col 4:3–6)

3.4
Our goal is conversion not coercion

There is a clear distinction between *proselytism* and *conversion* in the New Testament. Prior to the coming of Christ the Jewish people had a well-established process through which devout and God-seeking Gentiles could be admitted to the religion and community of Israel. In this way, Andrew Walls says, they were 'effectively de-cultured as Gentiles' and received into the faith as proselytes – 'to all outward appearances they became Jewish.'[94] The early church obviously understood this model but, as we have seen, chose to abandon it in favour of a new approach involving conversion. This clear break with Jewish tradition led to a situation in which Gentile converts to Christ were 'left to find a Christian lifestyle of their own within Hellenistic society under the guidance of the Holy Spirit.'[95] Christian converts, in contrast to Jewish proselytes, were not to be extracted from their culture; instead they were specifically called to remain within Greek society and to develop a pattern of discipleship within that context.

In fact, Andrew Walls says:

'It was their task to convert their society; convert it in the sense that they had to learn to keep turning their ways of thinking and doing things – which, of course, were Greek ways of thinking and doing things – towards Christ, opening them up to his influence. In this way, a truly Greek, truly Hellenistic type of Christianity was able to emerge.'[96]

> **Peter refused to impose on converts more than the central demands of Christian discipleship.**

This was a paradigm shift. The Jewish model of the expansion of the religious community (proselytisation) was replaced by a new model of mission – conversion. As David Smith explains in his book *Mission After Christendom*, 'The former practice sought to guarantee that new adherents adopted the patterns of belief and behaviour already established as normative within the believing community and to this end they were circumcised, immersed in water and systematically instructed in the Law of Moses … But when, following the outpouring of the Holy Spirit on his Gentile hearers, Peter proceeds immediately to baptise Gentiles as believers in Jesus, he deliberately bypasses the normal cultural barriers thrown grown up to preserve the internal purity of the covenant community and accepts Cornelius and his friends as Roman followers of Jesus of Nazareth.'[97]

The message was clear – conversion does not involve abandoning one's previous cultural identity, but rather a turning towards Jesus Christ from inside it. 'This is an astonishing move which makes possible a variety of forms of Christianity, each at home within its own cultural setting … as a result, Christianity is from its inception characterised by a cultural pluralism which permits the formation of churches reflecting human diversity and grants recognition to the insights into the mystery of Christ derived from the experience of faith in him within the various contexts.'[98]

3.5
New ways of being church

The implications of this for the church are enormous as Smith goes on to explain: 'In practice churches have usually employed the language of conversion while actually requiring people from other cultures and religions to become proselytes.'[99]

Peter refused to impose on converts more than the central demands of Christian discipleship. This groundbreaking principle is articulated throughout Paul's letters but has rarely been put into practice. Like the Judaisers in the New Testament, the church has often imposed on her 'converts' pre-packaged forms of church life, structure and discipleship which have had the effect of extracting them from their own communities and isolating them in such a way as to make it near impossible to witness to Christ from the inside of their cultures.

Malam Ibrahim, a devout Muslim scholar, lived in the city of Kano, in northern Nigeria. As the result of his studies, he slowly became convinced of the supreme importance of the prophet *Isa* (Jesus) within the *Qu'ran*. Ibrahim had no contact with Western Christianity or even any access to a copy of the New Testament. Yet by carefully and systematically studying every reference to Isa in the Qu'ran he came to believe that Jesus was greater than all the other prophets and therefore to be revered and followed. He began sharing his discoveries with fellow Muslims and in time gathered a group of followers around him who became known as *Isawa* – followers of Jesus. However, the group soon attracted the attention of the authorities and eventually he was arrested, tried and executed – impaled on a stake in Kano market.

But, the Isawa survived – indeed they grew stronger – a group of Muslims devoted to Jesus and now inspired by a

leader whose own death so clearly reflected Christ, who though Ibrahim had known only dimly, he had followed faithfully.[100]

Was Malam Ibrahim a contemporary Cornelius? David Smith believes that answering questions like these is vital in a pluralist society because 'devout adherents of other faiths are unlikely ever to get close to the Jesus of the Gospels as long as the lifestyle of evangelists, or the worship of churches shaped by Western individualism and modernisation, makes him appear to be the destroyer of all that is treasured within their traditions. The tragedy of the proselytising approach to mission is that it turns the gospel into 'bad news' … and short-circuits the revolutionary impact of the living Christ.'[101]

However, when Peter returned to Jerusalem from his time with Cornelius he found himself at the centre of a huge controversy and the object of much suspicion and severe criticism. The Jewish Christians wanted to guard the very boundaries which he had just ignored in order to set up a Gentile congregation. Peter's experience has been repeated over and over again throughout the history of cross-cultural evangelism and mission.

'Those who have broken new ground for the sake of Christ have found themselves carpeted by the guardians of orthodox faith,' Smith continues. 'The very survival of Christianity in Europe and America depends upon the emergence of men and women able to think new thoughts and devise new strategies at the real frontiers of mission today. But such people … are likely to face misunderstanding, criticism and serious opposition. Like Peter the Apostle and generations of pioneering, Spirit-led missionaries before them, those who are ready to confront the challenge posed by Western culture must not be surprised if they are accused of unorthoxdoxy, even heresy, or are verbally attacked by people who interpret their missionary vision as something liable to undermine the moral purity and integrity of the church of Jesus Christ.'[102]

Our God is the Universal God!

QUESTION TIME

1. In his book *Religion and Globalisation* sociologist David Lyons suggests: 'The cross may turn out to have more in common with the crescent than the Nike swoosh or the golden arches.'[103] Why do you think he said this? Do you think there is any truth in the suggestion?

2. Do you think 'evangelism' is an embarrassing word? Why?

3. The church has often imposed on her 'converts' pre-packaged forms of church life, structure and discipleship which have had the effect of extracting them from their own communities and isolating them in such a way as to make it near impossible to witness to Christ from the inside of their cultures. How do we avoid this?

4. Imagine the church in 2100. What does it look like?
   • in your community – the people, buildings, outreach
   • in our nation – the people, gatherings, publicity, spin
   • globally – mission, presence, impact

5. Peter had to learn the difficult lesson that faithfulness to scripture does not necessarily mean 'doing things the way that we have always done them.' Read Acts 10:34–36. What would this paradigm shift have meant for Peter's life, friendships and ministry?

FURTHER READING

Four Views on Salvation in a Pluralistic World by Dennis Okholm and Timothy Phillips (eds) (Zondervan, 1995) is a comprehensive roundup of the various positions on pluralism. Essays from John Hick, Clark Pinnock, Alister McGrath, Douglas Geivett and Gary Phillips outline the four main standpoints and each author is given the opportunity to respond to the others.

Christians and Muslims by Peter Riddell (IVP, 2004) examines the relationship between the world's two foremost religions. It addresses some of the most important questions the church needs to face at the start of the twenty-first century.

The Gospel in a Pluralist Society by Lesslie Newbigin (SPCK, 1989) is an excellent exploration of the challenges of mission in multi-faith communities.

The Bible and Other Faiths: Christian Responsibility in a World of Religions by Ida Glaser (IVP, 2005) explores biblical perspectives on other faiths – accessible, clear, extremely well researched. Helps us to understand religions and the way they affect people.

Dissonant voices: Religious Pluralism and the Question of Truth by Harold Netland (Apollos, 1991) is the classic work on pluralism.

Encountering Religious Pluralism: The challenge to the Christian Faith and Mission by Harold Netland (Apollos, 2001) traces the emergence of the pluralistic ethos that now challenges traditional Christian faith and mission.

Mark 2:1–12

Jesus Heals a Paralytic

A few days later, when Jesus again entered Capernaum, the people heard that he had come home. So many gathered that there was no room left, not even outside the door, and he preached the word to them. Some men came, bringing to him a paralytic, carried by four of them. Since they could not get him to Jesus because of the crowd, they made an opening in the roof above Jesus and, after digging through it, lowered the mat the paralysed man was lying on. When Jesus saw their faith, he said to the paralytic, "Son, your sins are forgiven."

Now some teachers of the law were sitting there, thinking to themselves, "Why does this fellow talk like that? He's blaspheming! Who can forgive sins but God alone?"

Immediately Jesus knew in his spirit that this was what they were thinking in their hearts, and he said to them, "Why are you thinking these things? Which is easier: to say to the paralytic, 'Your sins are forgiven,' or to say, 'Get up, take your mat and walk'? But that you may know that the Son of Man has authority on earth to forgive sins… ." He said to the paralytic, "I tell you, get up, take your mat and go home." He got up, took his mat and walked out in full view of them all. This amazed everyone and they praised God, saying, "We have never seen anything like this!"

The BIG ISSUE

Teaching Block 1
The Human God: The 'One of Us' God

1.1   What is Christology?

1.2   How do we know Jesus was a real man?

1.3   Jesus – the only normal human being

1.4   How do we really know that Jesus was God?

  1.4.1   Jesus' titles

  1.4.2   What did 'Messiah' mean?

1.4.3   Jesus the miracle worker

1.4.4   Was Jesus just another prophet?

1.4.5   Jesus the forgiver

1.4.6   Jesus commands the Holy Spirit

1.4.7   Jesus' resurrection

1.4.8   Jesus is Lord

QUESTION TIME

Teaching Block 2
The Human God: The Social God

2.1   Familiar but unknown

  2.1.1   The Son of God

  2.1.2   The Spirit of God

2.2   Knowing the unknowable

2.3   What does the Trinity mean for us?

2.4   Communities that mirror God

2.5   Churches that mirror God

QUESTION TIME

Teaching Block 3
The Human God: The Forgiving God

3.1   What is the atonement?

3.2   How does atonement work?

3.3   The way of the cross

3.4   Learning to forgive – A personal principle

3.5   Learning to forgive – A global principle

QUESTION TIME

FURTHER READING

The BIG ISSUE

On 30 April 1999, at the height of the NATO bombing of Serbia the president of the Czech Republic, Václav Havel, addressed both houses of the Canadian parliament. Havel used his speech to express his deep conviction that the greatest political challenge of the twenty-first century would be to ensure that all nation states submit to the rule of international law and uphold universal human rights. He concluded with these words:

'I have often asked myself why human beings have any rights at all. I have always come to the conclusion that human rights, human freedoms, and human dignity have their deepest roots somewhere outside the perceptible world. These values … make sense only in the perspective of the infinite and the eternal… . Allow me to conclude my remarks on the state and its probable role in future with the assertion that, while the state is a human creation, human beings are the creation of God.'[104]

Today we arrive at the very heart of the Christian faith: the human God. Here in a nutshell lies everything that makes Christianity unique. All of our deepest insights into the nature of God and humanity, human dignity and human rights (and responsibilities) both individual and communal are wrapped up in the person of Jesus.

The New Testament writers claim that Jesus is the 'image of the invisible God'. (2 Cor 4:4, Col 1:15–20) In other words

Jesus demonstrates what the *imago Dei* looks like in full flower. Or, to put it another way, it is only through Christ that we discover both what God is really like and what it is to be truly human.

We know that Jesus lived – no-one seriously argues with this. But beyond that, questions have always been asked about the church's belief that he is God. *The Da Vinci Code* – one of the most controversial and bestselling novels of the last few years – is now also set to become a Hollywood blockbuster starring Tom Hanks and Sir Ian McKellen. In the book, which already enjoys cult status, author Dan Brown suggests that the whole idea that Jesus is God and that he is part of a trinity was concocted by the church in order to keep itself in power. 'Jesus was viewed by his followers as a mortal prophet … a great and powerful man, but a man nonetheless.'[105]

So we need to address some basic questions about Jesus' humanity and his divinity.

- How do we know that Jesus really is God rather than just another prophet, guru or wise man?
- Did Jesus actually claim divinity for himself or did the church invent the story?
- The Bible never mentions the Trinity so why do Christians believe in it?
- Does the doctrine of the Trinity actually make any difference to Christians?

Teaching Block 1: The Human God: The 'One of Us' God

1.1
What is Christology?

The word Christology comes from two Greek words – 'Messiah' (*Christos*) and 'word' (*logos*) – which combine to mean 'the study of Christ'. The central theme of Christology is to understand how and why it was that

faith originated in Jesus of Nazareth as one and the same individual as God the Son – the second person of the Trinity.

'Christology is concerned … not only with unfolding the Christian community's confession of Christ, but above all with grounding it in the activity … of Jesus … Christology cannot take its point of departure from the confessions of the Reformation … nor [even] … the oldest primitive

4

Christian confession, the sentence *Içsous* (Christos) *Kyrios* ('Jesus is Lord').[106] (Wolfhart Pannenberg, *Jesus – God and Man*)

Our belief that Jesus is God must be grounded in, and substantiated by, the facts of the life of Jesus of Nazareth.

The claim of the incarnation is this: Jesus of Nazareth was fully man and, at one and the same time, fully God. If it is true it is the most profound event in the history of the world – God becomes a man and walks on the earth he has created. God comes to where we are. And, if it is true, it has huge implications for the whole way in which we understand and relate to God, for the way in which we think of ourselves, of others and the way in which we imagine society.

1.2
How do we know Jesus was a real man?

Gregory of Nazianzus (325–389) summed up the importance of Jesus' absolute humanity in a profound statement: 'What is not assumed cannot be redeemed.' In other words, if Jesus had not entered into the human experience fully, he could not have secured the redemption of humanity.

In order for the incarnation to successfully reconcile us to God, both Jesus' full humanity and divinity were essential components of his nature. Why? Because...

The first Christians had all personally known Jesus, his

'Unless God took on himself the whole of human nature at the incarnation, then the whole of human nature is not healed. If part of what it means to be a human being is left out of Jesus, then part of what it means to be a human being is not put right. If Jesus is not fully human, then our full humanity is still cut off from God.' (Michael Lloyd, *Café Theology*)[107]

family or his friends – they knew he was human. Their problem was all to do with coming to terms with how it was that he could be the eternal God. Our problem is often exactly the opposite. We are tempted to believe that although Jesus looked like an ordinary human on the outside, he wasn't really the same as us on the inside because he was God, and that being divine somehow added to his humanity and made him invincible; a kind of first century 'Superman' without the tights. Therefore, dealing with temptation was never going to be any problem for him. Jesus could have done 40 days, 40 weeks, 40 months or even 40 years without food (or water!) in the desert.

However, according to the Bible, in terms of his humanity, Jesus was different from us because he was *more* human than we are, not less so. Jesus was human in the very fullest possible sense. He aged, experienced hunger, thirst, pain, sorrow, tiredness, joy, pressure, tension, rejection, fear and anger – the full gamut of human feelings, needs and emotions. And he lived with all of the functions associated with his physicality – though it doesn't fit our stained-glass-window ideas of him, the consequences of eating and drinking were no less real for Jesus than for us. Furthermore, the Bible insists, Jesus was tempted to sin in exactly the same way as we are:

'He had to be made like his brothers in every way … Because he himself suffered when he was tempted, he is able to help those who are being tempted.' (Heb 2:17–18)

But was Jesus incapable of sin? Was he in the final analysis immune or what the scholars call 'impeccable'? A careful survey of the way in which the gospels and the letter to the Hebrews speak of Jesus leaves us in no doubt:

'Surely genuine temptations presuppose at least the possibility of moral failure? No one wants to suggest that Jesus' temptations were a mere charade, as if he simply went through the motions of being tempted to give us a good example, without feeling any pull whatsoever from

An old dilemma

If Jesus was fully human and fully divine, if he was incapable of sin, how could the temptation he faced be real?

So was Jesus *able not* to sin, or was he *not able* to sin

We know that Jesus never actually sinned. This is shown throughout the Gospels and stated explicitly in 1 John 3:5 'And in him is no sin' as well as in 1 John 2:1, Hebrews 7:2 and 2 Corinthians 5:21.

We know that Jesus faced real temptation, specifically for forty days in the wilderness (Luke 4:2) and in the Garden of Gethsemane (Matt 26) but throughout the Gospels. Jesus was 'tempted in every way, just as we are—yet was without sin' (Heb 4:15).

We also know that 'God cannot be tempted by evil' (James 1:13).

Was Jesus incapable of sin?

If Jesus' human nature had existed by itself, independent of his divine nature, then in theory it would have been able to sin. But Jesus' human nature and divine nature only ever existed united in one person. An act of sin would have involved the whole person.

If Jesus as a person had sinned, then God himself would have sinned, and he would have ceased to be God. That is clearly impossible because of the infinite holiness of God's nature.

Therefore it was ultimately not possible for Jesus to have sinned. The union of his human and divine natures would have prevented it.

So how could the temptations Jesus faced be real?

When Jesus was tempted in the wilderness, he refused to turn stones into bread. He refused to meet temptation to sin by his divine power, but faced it on the strength of his human nature alone. Jesus always depended perfectly on God the Father and the Holy Spirit, as we should, and the moral strength of his divine nature was always there, but he did not rely on his divine nature to make it easier for him to face temptation.

In 1988 cinemas around the world were picketed by thousands of evangelical Christians. The film they rallied against was Martin Scorsese's *The Last Temptation of Christ*, based on Nikos Kazantzakis' 1955 novel of the same name.

The film, an obviously fictional take on the gospel stories, depicts a very human Jesus who struggles with doubt and temptation. In one scene, while hanging on the cross, Jesus struggles mentally with sexual temptation. It was this scene that caused most controversy and inspired so many people to protest outside cinemas showing the film. It was considered blasphemy to suggest that Jesus was tempted sexually and heresy to suppose that it was not easy for him to resist any temptation he faced.

But the great irony is that the most obvious problem with Scorsese's film was psychological rather than theological. Many of us find it difficult to believe that Jesus would have faced sexual temptation while on the cross, but, as he was fully human, he would have in the rest of his life.

temptation. How could he have been subject to temptation and yet incapable of moral error.' (Gerald O'Collins)[108]

1.3
Jesus – the only normal human being

'If Jesus is God living a human life, then we have, in him, the designer's blueprint for how human beings are meant to live. So if we want to know what it would look like to be completely human – human in a way that is unmarred and unscarred by the myriad ways in which we habitually distort our humanity – then it is to Jesus that we must turn.' (Lloyd, *Café*)[109]

We bear the *imago Dei* – we are created to be in relationship with God – but that relationship has been distorted by sin. However, sin is not normal. It is something that we all do, but it is not normal because it isn't what we were originally designed to do.

In Jesus, we have the model or example of how to live life as we were intended to. Jesus resisted – he would not cave in, even under the full power and force of the most intense temptation, to sin and selfishness. C.S. Lewis illustrates exactly this point in his book *Mere Christianity* when he comments that we will often complain that we buckle under temptation simply because we find it so intense that we cannot resist. 'You just don't know how difficult it is for me,' we protest. But, says Lewis, we make a huge mistake if we imply that a person who doesn't give in to temptation obviously hasn't felt its power with the same force as we did. It is only the reed that stands against the storm and doesn't

The politics of incarnation

Various Christian friends asked me, "Why on earth do you want to be in politics? It's full of sharks!" But, the world was full of sharks when Jesus walked this earth too and that didn't stop him. And I suppose that in the end that is what incarnation is all about.

So, what does it mean to try and live like Jesus in the political world?

Well, to start with Jesus was a servant. Our society is still intensely hierarchical and we see plenty of this in the political structures of our day. But the capacity to serve selflessly is at the heart of the incarnation. It's a challenge, but perhaps it's also the reason that there is a higher percentage of Christians in politics than in the population at large, about 20% distributed across all parties.

Politics produces laws which are designed to make the world a better place but just changing the laws of the land will never solve complex problems. I do not believe for example that restoring the married couple's tax allowance would stop the divorce rate from rising. The introduction of anti-social behaviour orders is an attempt to crack down on the rising trend of selfish and damaging behaviour in society but it does not address the underlying cause. Why do young people feel it is alright to spray graffiti over other people's property, drink themselves to oblivion and verbally abuse those who challenge them? However, on the other hand, I do believe that politicians send signals by the laws they pass.

Jesus constantly challenged the legalistic views of the political leaders in his day and invited them to look deeper – to see the heart of the matter. Where was the sense in letting a donkey die down the bottom of a well just because it was a Sabbath day? In the same way today's Christian politicians must resist knee-jerk 'party politics' and have the courage to point to how God's heart would have us respond.

So, every day I need to ask that question: 'what would Jesus do?' This is what any and every Christian vocation is all about - being called to be like, and speak like Jesus, a kind of mini version of the word incarnate.

And, part of it for those of us in politics it is to speak with Christ's Spirit whichever side of that dispatch box we stand.

Caroline Spelman MP

break that ever feels the full power of the wind – never the one that snaps and lays down flat!'

Though our goal is to be Christ-like, it feels an unfair task; after all, we think, he was God! However, in truth, it is not Jesus' divinity that we are called to emulate; we are not asked to aim at divinity! Instead it is the true humanity of Christ that we are called to follow – living life as we were intended to do, in relationship with our heavenly Father.

1.4
How do we really know that Jesus was God?

Christians believe that Jesus was God. But where do we get this from? How would you explain the evidence for this claim to a Jewish neighbour, or a Muslim friend?

John's Gospel is a good place to start. It is rich in Christology and contains perhaps the most important passage which discusses the idea of incarnation. 'In the beginning was the Word, and the Word was with God, and the Word was God' (John 1:1) and 'The Word became flesh and made his dwelling among us.' (John 1:14) Having

What does the Old Testament say about Christ?

In the Gospel of John, Philip tells Nathanael, 'We have found the one Moses wrote about in the Law, and about whom the prophets also wrote—Jesus of Nazareth' (John 1:45), and Jesus himself claims that 'If you believed Moses, you would believe me, for he wrote about me' (John 5:46). On the road to Emmaus Jesus began with Moses and the prophets and explained to the disciples 'what was said in all the Scriptures concerning himself.' (Luke 24:25–27)

So what were the Old Testament Scriptures that pointed to Jesus?

There were many, but among the most important passages were:

Deuteronomy 18 – 'The Lord your God will raise up for you a prophet like me from among your own brothers. You must listen to him … I will raise up for them a prophet like you from among their brothers; I will put my words in his mouth, and he will tell them everything I command them.' (Deut 18:15–20)

Towards the end of Moses' life, God promises to raise up a prophet like him who will lead the people. This referred to the immediate succession of leaders after Moses, but Jews believed this also pointed to the Messiah, and Christians believe there is a unique fulfilment in Christ. In his sermon on the day of Pentecost in Acts 3:22–26, Peter quotes this

same passage and claims that Jesus was the fulfilment of this promise.

The book of Isaiah – The people of Israel are described here as God's servant, with a task of declaring his greatness in the world. In places this vision focuses on a particular individual, the Lord's servant. These include Isaiah 42:1–7; 49:1–7, 50:4–9, 52:13–53:12 and are sometimes referred to as the Servant Songs. At the start of his ministry Jesus reads from Isaiah 61:1,2 and makes the staggering claim that 'this Scripture is fulfilled in your hearing.' (Luke 4:18–21)

The Psalms – Certain psalms seem to point specifically to Christ as 'his Anointed One'. These include Psalm 2:2, 18:50, 84:9, 132:10,17.

Daniel 9:25–27 – Jesus specifically refers to Daniel's vision of the Son of Man coming on the clouds of heaven during his trial at the Sanhedrin, and this is taken as a claim to be God, and evidence of blasphemy against him. (Matt 26:64)

This is only part of the picture. There are many other ways that the Old Testament story points towards and is fulfilled by the coming of Christ. For example, Chris Wright explains how all the major functions of YHWH in the Old Testament of Creator, Ruler, Judge, Saviour are attributed to Jesus in a remarkable way in the New Testament.

has seen me has seen the Father. How can you say, 'Show us the Father'?"

However, if John has a developed Christology, it is sometimes claimed that the synoptic Gospels (Matthew, Mark and Luke), which were all written much earlier, do not. The critics claim that John's writing reflects or writes back into the gospel what had by that time become the belief of the church rather than what Jesus originally taught about himself. So, do the first three gospels also teach that Jesus explicitly claimed to be divine?

established this foundation the Gospel of John continues to record the statements of Jesus, which press home the point:

John 5:17–18: Jesus said to them, "My Father is always at his work to this very day, and I, too, am working." For this reason the Jews tried all the harder to kill him; not only was he breaking the Sabbath, but he was even calling God his own Father, making himself equal with God.

John 5:22: "Moreover, the Father judges no-one, but has entrusted all judgment to the Son."

John 8:58–59: "I tell you the truth," Jesus answered, "before Abraham was born, I am!" At this, they picked up stones to stone him, but Jesus hid himself, slipping away from the temple grounds.

John 10:30–31: "I and the Father are one." Again the Jews picked up stones to stone him, …

John 10:38–39: "But if I do it, even though you do not believe me, believe the miracles, that you may know and understand that the Father is in me, and I in the Father." Again they tried to seize him, but he escaped their grasp.

John 14:9: Jesus answered: "Don't you know me, Philip, even after I have been among you such a long time? Anyone who

1.4.1
Jesus' titles

We tend to believe that the way we know that Jesus was God is because of the titles he adopted. 'Son of Man', 'Son of God', 'Messiah' and 'Christ' were all titles that were applied to Jesus, either by himself or by his followers. However, it is critical to understand that none of these (of themselves) actually confer divinity in their original sense. What is more, they wouldn't have suggested it to those who originally heard them used of Jesus.

'Christ' is the Greek translation of the Hebrew word for 'Messiah', which means 'Anointed One'; and the two other designations, 'Son of Man' and 'Son of God', are closely related to it. So, for instance, the New Testament scholar Howard Marshall claims that 'although … "Christ" developed into a name for Jesus (e.g. Rom 5:6; 1 Cor 1:12, 17; Heb 3:6, 9:11), [originally] the word is basically a description or title of a person with a particular function.' He adds that the Jews used it in several ways but most importantly it was 'applied to the king, who is regarded as standing in a special relationship (on behalf of his people) to God.'[110]

> It is almost impossible to overestimate the Messiah's prestige and status in Jewish eyes.

N.T. Wright agrees, saying: 'Messiah or Christ, does not mean 'the/a divine one … it is very misleading to use the words as shorthands for the divine nature or being of Jesus.' Likewise, 'the phrase 'son of God', is systematically misleading. Because in pre- or non-Christian Judaism its primary referent is either Israel or the Messiah.'[111]

Wolfhart Pannenburg says: 'The title 'Son of God' was connected in ancient Israel with the inauguration of the king, which occurred as adoption by Yahweh (Psa 2:7). It implied there, as well as in the earliest Christian community, a clear subordination [rather than equality] of the messiah to God.'[112]

'So, when Peter says to Jesus 'You are the Messiah', and when Caiaphas says the same words as an ironic question, neither of them should be understood as either stating or asking whether Jesus thinks he is the incarnate second person of the Trinity. Subsequent Christian use of the word 'Christ' … and indeed of the phrase 'Son of God', as though they were 'divine' titles has, to say the least, not helped people to grasp this point; but grasped it must be if we are to understand Jesus in his historical context.'[113]

But what about the phrase 'Son of Man' – the most commonly used 'self-designation' by Jesus – which occurs over fifty times in the Gospels, excluding parallel forms of the same sayings? It too is linked to the role of the Messiah and is used first in the Old Testament in Daniel 7:13, who has a vision of 'one like a son of man' who was given dominion and glory and kingdom, that all peoples, nations and languages should serve him. When Jesus makes an unmistakable reference to this vision in his trial before the Sanhedrin, this is taken as clear evidence of blasphemy.

Howard Marshall suggests that its primary reference is to 'the leader of the saints of the Most High', because 'he can properly be said to represent them', but like 'son of God' it can also be used 'as a symbol for the [whole] people of God … as we may say that Britannia symbolizes the British people.'[114]

The phrase 'Son of Man' is used in three different ways by Jesus: sometimes speaking of his earthly activity, sometimes speaking of his sufferings, and sometimes speaking of his glory, and thereby explicitly hinting at his claim to be God.

1.4.2
What did 'Messiah' mean?

In the first century all Israel was awaiting the Messiah. There was a huge sense of anticipation surrounding his arrival. It is, in fact, almost impossible to overestimate the Messiah's prestige and status in Jewish eyes. However, the task of this Messiah was to be a warrior leader who would defeat their enemies and set Israel free from oppression. Just as we might expect our political leaders to deal with education, the health service and the economy, so the Jews expected the genuine Messiah to deliver on a number of fundamental issues, including defeating Rome, bringing them independence and restoring the Temple. So, for instance, says Howard Marshall, 'When Simon bar Koseba led the Jews in their second war of independence against Rome (AD 132–135) he was hailed by a leading rabbi as "the King, the Messiah".'[115]

Jesus' claim to divinity was consistent, clear and unambiguous, but even he in applying the title Messiah to himself was not claiming to be divine. He was instead declaring to Israel that he was God's agent for change.

Howard Marshall points out that the term 'Christ' is used rarely by Jesus of himself before his death, and adds that it is almost as though he was reticent to use the title until he 'had made it clear that he is a crucified Messiah, and he cannot be known as such except by those who are prepared to suffer self-denial and tread the path of humble discipleship.'[116]

In this way, he says, Jesus 'sought to fulfil the Messianic role in a new way.' 'I'm the Messiah, I'll set you free, but not in the way that you are expecting.'

Though our desire to identify Jesus as God incarnate cannot be satisfied in simple reference to his assumed titles, each of them not only adds new depth and dimension to our understanding of the impact that he made in his original context but also of what it means for us to worship him today as the true Messiah – not only for Israel but for the whole world.

4

'Miracles were not accepted without question in antiquity. Graeco-Roman writers were often reluctant to ascribe "miraculous" events [even] to the gods, and offered alternative explanations ... so it is a mistake to write off the miracles of Jesus as the result of naivety and gullibility of people in the ancient world.' (Marshall, *Origins*)

It is telling that there is no debate, either within the biblical text or from contemporary sources outside it, about whether Jesus actually did miracles. The ongoing dispute was, instead, about where the power for them came from – did it come from God (Matt 12:28) as Jesus claimed, from Satan (Matt 12:24) as the Pharisees suggested, or from his own 'magical powers'? The comments of Celsus, a philosopher and pagan critic of Christianity, are revealing. About the year 180 he wrote as follows:

1.4.3
Jesus the miracle worker

If Jesus' titles do not automatically confer divinity upon him, is the fact that he was a miracle worker a sign of his deity?

'Christians get the power they seem to possess by pronouncing the names of certain daemons and incantations ... It was by magic that he [Jesus] was able to do the miracles which he appears to have done.'[117]

'There are seventeen accounts of healings in the Gospels, including three of revivification [bringing someone back to life]; there are six accounts of exorcisms. Eight further traditions are usually referred to as 'nature miracles'. These numbers do not include parallel passages or the many references to miracles in summary passages. The bald statistics confirm the prominence of miracles in the Gospels.' (Marshall, *Origins*)

Celsus did not doubt that both Jesus and his followers performed miracles, but he attributed them to magical powers.

It is wrong, however, to assume that Jesus' miracles necessarily prove his divinity. In fact, to do so also entirely misses the point:

First, we should not blindly accept that Jesus did miracles at all. We all have friends who simply dismiss them as ridiculous stories. 'It's impossible,' they say. 'Jesus' miracles are simply stories he told turned by the gospel writers into real events to impress their readers and boost Jesus' credibility in an age when people were easier to take in.'

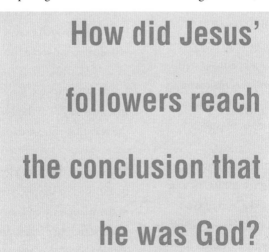

How did Jesus' followers reach the conclusion that he was God?

'The powers of Jesus to heal and to exorcise were not unique. He gave his own disciples authority to heal and to exorcise (Mark 6:7, 13; Matt 10:1). Jesus himself refers to other exorcists who were able to cast out demons (Matt 12:27, Luke 11:19). There are [also] reports of Jewish miracle workers who lived about the time of Jesus, though they are not common.' (Graham Stanton, *Message and Miracles*)

Such scepticism is not new, however.

The critical thing about Jesus referring to other exorcists and giving his disciples the authority to heal the sick and to drive out demons is that those things cannot then be held as conclusive evidence that he was God. If all his disciples could, and should, be doing these same miracles (albeit in his name) it is clear that they are a function of the in-breaking kingdom of God, rather than actions proving divinity. In his miracles Jesus was once again showing us what it meant to be fully human – not attempting to prove that he was fully God.

Some have argued that the 'nature' miracles – walking on water, calming the storm, feeding the thousands from a small packed lunch – break this rule. But on the biblical evidence one would have to conclude not. When Peter saw Jesus walking on the water (Matt 14:22-33) he climbed out of the boat and walked towards Jesus. We know that it was not Jesus as God keeping him up with some sort of divine beam, because Peter's own fear and lack of faith caused him to start to sink. It was Peter the man that made a few steps on the surface of the water, and it was Jesus the man that walked over to help him back into the boat.

True humanity it seems has dominion over nature in perhaps unexpected ways. That Jesus exercised that dominion does not serve as evidence of his divinity, but rather, once again, his humanity. The miracles show 'that Jesus actually achieves what human beings have both the capacity to do and were originally created to do. He is living out our potential … It is Jesus Christ, then, who is the true image of God.' (Graham McFarlane, *Why Do You Believe What You Believe About Jesus?*)[118]

In the words of the Chinese Christian leader Watchman Nee, 'Jesus was the only normal human being'.

So, how did Jesus' followers reach the conclusion that he was God? How did they become so convinced that he was divine that they were willing to, and in the majority of cases did, die for their belief?

1.4.4
Was Jesus just another prophet?

Jesus spoke with tremendous authority. His hearers recognised it instantly. 'The people were all so amazed that they asked each other, "What is this? A new teaching – and with authority!"' (Mark 1:27) Jesus did not speak in the manner of a prophetic spokesperson for God; he talked as if he were divine. He spoke as if he already was, in John's terminology, the word of God.

'Jesus spoke not as if he were speaking on "behalf of God" (he did not say, as the prophets had done "Thus says the Lord"), "but as if he were divine", delivering the truth to human beings. Nowhere in the Gospels does it say anything like "the word of the Lord came to Jesus."' (Stephen Davis, *Was Jesus Mad, Bad or God?*)[119]

Instead, Jesus would begin his statements with 'amen, amen', that is 'but I say to you', which was unheard of, an amazing claim to his own authority. Jesus puts his teaching on a level with the Old Testament teaching. 'Heaven and earth will pass away, but my words will never pass away' (Mark 13:31, but look also at Matt 5:18). He even assumed for himself the authority to reinterpret and overrule Old Testament Law. So, for instance, in the Sermon on the Mount he quotes and then corrects the Mosaic teaching (see Matt 5:21-48; Mark 2:23-8), something that no mere human being could do. So stark is this characteristic that as Jacob Neusner, a contemporary Jewish scholar, complains Jesus' attitude towards the law makes him want to ask: 'Who do you think you are? God?'[120]

1.4.5
Jesus the forgiver

Jesus also implicitly taught his own divinity by assuming for himself the divine prerogative to forgive sins (Mark 2:5-12; Luke 7:48). All humans own the right to forgive sins that have been committed against them, but only God can forgive sins!

'The authority that Jesus claims presupposes a solidarity with God, that no other man has. What Jesus does is blasphemy unless it comes from special authority. He claims this authority for himself … For this reason God's forgiveness is a present event in his words of consolation in his eating with sinners.' (Pannenburg, *Jesus*)

4

1.4.6
Jesus commands the Holy Spirit

Jesus' relationship with God the Father and the Spirit was certainly a special one – consider the account of his baptism (Luke 3:22). But after his death and resurrection, this special relationship enters a new phase. Before his death Jesus promises: 'I tell you the truth: It is for your good that I am going away. Unless I go away, the Counsellor will not come to you; but if I go, I will send him to you.' (John 16:7) But after his resurrection he delivers on those promises and proves his point.

'Before his resurrection and ascension Jesus could be seen merely as another inspired man. This cannot be the case after his resurrection … this is the staggering point of the entire New Testament. If Jesus is Lord of the Spirit then it means he has a unique relationship with God. Remember God is previously understood to be the Lord of the Spirit. Now Jesus is being accorded similar status.' (Graham McFarlane, *Why Do You Believe What You Believe About the Holy Spirit?*)[121]

If we understand the Spirit to be the breath of God as the Old Testament does in 'The Spirit of God has made me; the breath of the Almighty gives me life' (Job 33:4), who else but God could exert control over that breath? That Jesus could direct the Holy Spirit (Acts 1:1-8) speaks clearly of his divine status.

1.4.7
Jesus' resurrection

For all his followers Jesus' death was an utter tragedy, a humiliation – the end of the road. They had trusted him and now this. To a first-century Jew the idea of a 'crucified Messiah' was an oxymoron. A dead Messiah was no Messiah. A crucified Jesus stripped naked, gasping for breath, for water and for dignity, would not speak of atonement or liberation – instead it was an unmitigated disaster! To the first-century Jewish mind the concept that Jesus, who was nailed to a tree, could also be the promised Messiah was deeply shocking. In fact, it demanded a complete theological rethink.

'Death is the logical and chronological consequence of "sin" and [biblically] signifies our ultimate independence from God.' (Graham McFarlane)[122]

'The wages of sin is death,' Paul writes in Romans 6:23. So how could the Messiah die? But more than that, the nature of the death suffered by Jesus on the cross only added to the problem. In Deuteronomic law death by hanging on a tree symbolised the victim's status before God.

'If anyone guilty of a capital offence is put to death and the body is hung on a tree, you must not leave the body on the tree overnight. Be sure to bury it that same day, because anyone who is hung on a tree is under God's curse.' (Deut 21:22–23)

The Messiah was supposed to uphold the law – if a potential Messiah were crucified (hung on a tree) he was cursed by God under the law. The two concepts – 'messiah-hood' and 'death by crucifixion' – were simply not compatible!

Justin Martyr (died c.165) recorded the baffled reaction of cultured Jews. Their monotheistic faith and sense of the intrinsic otherness of God made them judge it 'incredible' and 'impossible' to think of God deigning to be born a human being and to end up dying on a cross.[123]

You only have to hear the mocking taunts that rained down on Jesus while he hung on the cross to understand that.

Tony Campolo tells a now well-known story of a preaching convention at his home church where his senior pastor spoke.

It was a simple sermon, Campolo recalls. It started softly, but it slowly built in volume and intensity until the entire congregation was completely involved.

"It's Friday," Tony's pastor whispered. "Jesus is arrested in the garden where He was praying. But Sunday's coming!"

"It's Friday," he began again, raising his voice slightly. "The disciples are hiding and Peter's denying that he knows the Lord. But Sunday's coming!"

"It's Friday," he repeated louder again. "Jesus is standing before the high priest of Israel, silent as a lamb. But Sunday's coming!"

"It's Friday. Jesus is beaten, mocked and spat upon." At this point the preacher paused and looked out across the congregation who all responded simultaneously with the cry, "But Sunday's coming!"

That was it, Tony says, he had them. Now each clause of his sermon just got louder and louder and the response from the crowd grew correspondingly in volume and enthusiasm. "It's Friday. Those Roman soldiers are flogging our Lord with a leather scourge that has bits of bones and glass and metal, tearing at his flesh. But Sunday's coming!"

"It's Friday. Jesus stands firm as they press the crown of thorns down into his brow. But Sunday's coming."

"It's Friday. See him walking to Calvary, the blood dripping from his body. See the cross crashing down on his back as he stumbles beneath the load. It's Friday; but Sunday's a coming."

"It's Friday. See those Roman soldiers driving the nails into the feet and hands of my Lord. Hear my Jesus cry, 'Father, forgive them.' It's Friday; but Sunday's coming."

"It's Friday. Jesus is hanging on the cross, bloody and dying. It's Friday, but Sunday's coming."

"It's Friday. The sky grows dark, the earth begins to tremble and Jesus cries out, 'My God, My God. Why hast thou forsaken me?' What a horrible cry. It's Friday, but Sunday's coming."

"It's Friday. And Jesus is dead and his followers are beaten." Silence descended on the church. People looked at the pastor. They looked at Campolo. They looked at each other. And then as with one voice they shouted out; "It's Friday – but Sunday's coming!"

'"He saved others," they said, "but he can't save himself! Let this Christ, this King of Israel, come down now from the cross, that we may see and believe."' (Mark 15:31-32) Even his followers had reminded him of this sobering fact when he tried to tell them about his forthcoming death: 'We have heard from the Law that the Christ will remain forever, so how can you say, "The Son of Man must be lifted up"?' (John 12:34) And as far as the Jewish authorities were concerned the purpose of nailing Jesus to a cross was to publicly state, 'Here he is, this would-be Messiah of yours: this is what happens to failed Messiahs!'

Of course, the voice of millions of Christians down through the centuries would argue that this simply wasn't true. However, as the theologian Lesslie Newbigin has pointed out, we all wear cultural spectacles that colour the way we see the world – but because they are worn on the inside of our heads it's harder to remove them! In the case of the cross, we view it through post-resurrection eyes and perhaps via our already developed faith in Jesus as Saviour and Lord. But for those who had followed Jesus around the towns and villages of Judea, and for the authorities who had plotted against him, their cultural spectacles meant they could see only one thing – a crucified Jesus; a failed Messiah; a dead rebel, cursed by men and cursed by God. He may have promised much, but in the end he simply failed to deliver.

'However, the fact that God raised Jesus from the dead means that this relationship between Law and Messiah has been turned on its head.' (Graham McFarlane, *Jesus*)

Jesus did die under the law, cursed by the law, and under

the judgement of God. The law itself clearly displays God's intentions and purposes, that sin should be judged. It is remarkable that Paul sees the law as having been fulfilled in the crucifixion.

McFarlane goes on to explain: 'The resurrection of Jesus from the dead ... shows that Jesus was indeed telling the truth about himself. He really was from God. It also proved that he did speak and act with an absolute authority that came only from God ... The resurrection, then, reveals the true identity of Jesus. Through resurrection God vindicates Jesus' pre-Easter activity and speech. It is not that the resurrection makes Jesus something he was not before. Rather, it makes public something that was clear to only a few prior to his resurrection.'

Now to say that Jesus 'was the "Son of God" was to ... acknowledge him to be God's actual representative on earth, to whom the same homage and obedience would be due as if one were suddenly in the presence of God himself ... It was only after his death and resurrection to the right hand of God that ... Jesus could be acknowledged ... as Son of God.'[124]

1.4.8
Jesus is Lord

The cross without the resurrection is a bitter blow, not just for the original followers of Jesus, the people of Israel, but for all humanity and for the whole of creation. Its message is violence wins, might is right, the weak will always be oppressed, downtrodden and abused by the powerful. But the events of the first Easter turn the tables. The God of love takes the powers of darkness and evil on their own terms

and wins. There is hope in the universe. 'You can trust me,' cries Jesus.

'Jesus' unity with God was not ... established by the claim implied in his pre-Easter appearance, but only by his resurrection from the dead.' (Pannenburg, *Jesus*)

The resurrection demonstrates that Jesus is God's Anointed One, God's Christ and the true Son of God.

So the first Christians begin to refer to Jesus as God (see Rom 9:5; Titus 2:13; Heb 1:8; 2 Pet 1:1), and raise the cry *Içsous Kyrios* – 'Jesus is Lord' (Rom 1:4, 10:9; 1 Cor 12:3). They also began to recognise how Old Testament texts addressed to Yahweh applied to Jesus. For instance, in Philippians 2:10–11 Jesus is portrayed in language taken from Isaiah 45:22–25 where every knee shall bow and every tongue confess. The author of Hebrews quotes Psalm 102:25, which speaks about the work of the Lord in creation and applies it to Christ. 'In the beginning you laid the foundations of the earth, and the heavens are the work of your hands.' And in 1 Corinthians Paul quotes the *Shema* and inserts Jesus into this foundational text of Judaism:

'Yet for us there is but one God, the Father, from whom all things came and for whom we live; and there is but one Lord, Jesus Christ, through whom all things came and through whom we live.' (1 Cor 8:6)

QUESTION TIME

1. It is not Jesus' divinity that we are called to emulate, instead it is the true humanity of Christ that we are called to follow. How do we do this more fully?

2. 'It's Friday but Sunday is coming.' In what areas of your life do you need Sunday to come? How can we wait well when life feels stuck on endless Saturdays?

3. In what ways is Jesus a different kind of Messiah to that which was expected? Read Matthew 21 and consider what the passage says to us about Jesus?

Teaching Block 2: The Human God: The Social God

2.1.
Familiar but unknown

'Hear, O Israel, the Lord our God, the Lord is one,' states the *Shema*. Therefore the slow realisation that Jesus was the Son of God who could command the Holy Spirit was truly mind-boggling to the first Christian thinkers.

'[We know] that early second-century writers were already noticing, analysing, and struggling with the implications of the Hebrew scriptures, apostolic testimony, and the church's worship in the attempt to understand God's nature and work.[125]

However, the new data they had in the person and work of Christ took a long time to digest. How could God be one if there appeared to be three elements in play?

'As the Christian community worshipped, studied, prayed, and meditated it increasingly realised that the God whom it encountered in Jesus Christ was mysterious and complex in a manner that defied human comprehension and linguistic analysis.' (Olsen & Hall, *Trinity*)

No reading of the Old Testament on its own will ever reveal the Trinity. However, in the light of the revelation through Jesus when the interpreters began to work back to the Old Testament from the claim that '*whoever has seen me has seen the Father*' (John 14:9), from his commanding of the Spirit, from his unilateral acts of forgiveness etc., they found themselves in mysteriously familiar territory.

The leading thinkers of the first four centuries argued over the implications of their radical belief that 'Jesus is Lord' – and it was out of this dialogue and debate that the doctrine of the Trinity was set to grow.

'Their conclusions were encapsulated [finally] in a succession of creedal statements, at once precise and pregnant, which serve as both boundary-markers and

starting-points for Christological reflection today.' (Donald Macleod, *The Person of Christ*)[126]

2.1.1
The Son of God

The first dispute regarding the relationship of Jesus to God was ignited by Arius' attempt to protect the absolute uniqueness of God. Because of this he claimed that the Father must have at some point in the distant past created the pre-existent Son.

However, in the judgement of others 'the future of Christianity as a religion was at stake. If Christ were not [eternally] God, he could not be the revelation of God. If Christ were not God, men had not been redeemed by God. If Christ were not God, believers were not united to God. Above all, if Christ were not God, Christians had no right to worship him. Indeed, if they did so, they were reverting to pagan superstition and idolatry.' (Macleod, *Person*)

So in order to combat Arianism (*see box 'Two Popular Errors' on page 85*) the first Ecumenical Church Council was convened in 325 in Nicaea. Here the church unequivocally affirmed the full deity of Jesus as the 'eternally begotten' Son of God who was substantially the same (made out of the same stuff) as the Father.

2.1.2
The Spirit of God

The second theological dispute, which emerged in the aftermath of Nicaea, also had its roots in Arius' teaching. Just as he had taught that the Son was the first creature of the Father, his followers theorised that the Holy Spirit was the first creature of the Son. This debate reached its climax in 381, when at the second Ecumenical Council held in Constantinople the status of the Holy Spirit was debated.

(*Sabellianism – See Box 'Two Popular Errors' on page 85*). The Greek speaking 'Cappadocian (or 'Desert') Fathers' – Basil of Caesarea, Gregory of Nyssa, and Gregory of Nazianzus – birthed the ingenious idea that God is one *ousia* (being) but three *hypostases* (realities) whilst Tertullian, whose first language was Latin, formulated the Trinity as three *personae* (persons) and one *substantia* (substance).

However, the Trinity is famously unfathomable. Whatever images we choose in illustration are frustrating in their limitations – whether we take the cloverleaf (it's all one thing, but has three distinct segments) or the natures of H^2O (solid/ice, liquid/water and gas/steam – one substance in three different forms) we still fail to grasp fully the mystery of who God is.

In *Café Theology*, Michael Lloyd asks four questions of those struggling to grasp the doctrine of the Trinity:

- Why would we expect the infinite, eternal God to be easily grasped by our minds, which are finite? After all, we don't say, 'Quantum Mechanics is so hard to understand, it can't be right!'
- Wouldn't we expect the God who made the rich, complex, incomprehensible and yet surprisingly knowable world to have a corresponding richness, complexity, diversity and delightfully explorable depth? If his mind conceived the complexities of creation, is he not likely to be less fathomable than they?
- Doesn't the doctrine of the Trinity have precisely the ring of something that comes from beyond human understanding rather than something that was engendered by it? If the map formulated by those who drew up this doctrine is unexpected and baffling to us, might that not be because the terrain they were attempting to map was unexpected and baffling to them?
- If we found the revelation of God's nature easy to understand and assimilate and accept, might that not mean that it was adding nothing to what we already knew and believed?

'Whereas the first ecumenical council of Nicaea in 325 had been content to confess belief in the Holy Spirit by the simple affirmation 'and in the Holy Spirit', the second ecumenical council inserted into the creed … certain phrases functionally equivalent to defining the deity of the third person of the Trinity in the way that Nicaea had done in respect to the second, the Son.' (Geoffrey Wainwright, *The Holy Spirit*)[127]

Thus what is popularly known as the Nicene Creed, but was substantially the work of the Constantinople Council, announced:

> And [we believe] in the Holy Spirit, the Lord and Life-Giver,
> Who proceeds from the Father,
> Who with the Father and the Son together is worshipped and glorified,
> Who has spoken through the prophets.[128]

2.2
Knowing the unknowable

However, though the parameters of the church's understanding of the Trinity were now set, neither Ecumenical Council had explained *how* the three persons comprise one God. The search was for some kind of middle ground between the error of teaching three gods (tri-theism) and the equally suspect idea that the three persons are merely modes of the revelation of the one God

Any talk about God should be deeply challenging. But rather than being discouraged by that complexity, especially when considering the Trinity – the very essence and nature of God himself – we should be inspired.

2.3
What does the Trinity mean for us?

It is often said that the most profound theological statement in the whole Bible is that 'God is love' (1 John 4:8). However, the truth is that were God a single person, if he were one rather than 'three and one', we could not know him as love.

'Self-love cannot be true charity, supreme love requires another, equal to the lover, who is the recipient of that love, and because supreme love is received as well as given, it must be a shared love, in which each person loves and is loved by the other.' (Grenz, *Social*)

If God is just one and not three, then he is not intrinsically love, because until he created the world, he would have had nothing to love.

'For "most" of eternity he would not have been involved in a loving relationship. He would be dependent upon the world to provide an object for his love.' (Lloyd, *Café*)

It is only because the Father, Son and Spirit respond to each other in constantly loving relationships that we can say that the very nature of God is love.

As Derek Tidball comments, 'Love is not a quality that God possesses, but the essence of God himself. It is not a minor attribute that characterises God on occasions, but the very heart of God, his essential being. It is not a component part of God, but his very nature. Before God is anything else, he is love.'[129]

In essence the doctrine of the Trinity tells us that God is a community. Three persons – Father, Son and Spirit – one in substance (or essence) but actually defined by their relationships to one another. God exists as a 'triunity' of persons. The eternally pre-existent Jesus was not born within the Trinity – there was never a time when God was two persons expecting a third. God, then, is in constant internal relationship. The Father is in relationship with the Son by the Spirit and cannot be the Father other than through this relation-ship, since without the Son he would not be the Father. The profound truth is that God is a society within himself. God, because he is three, is by his very nature social.

'God is a fellowship of persons whose orientation is entirely to the other. The notion of there being three persons in God is problematic for us, because we think that person means individual in the modern sense of one whose being is defined over against, even in opposition to, other individu-als … The Trinitarian notion of person does incorporate one aspect of the notion of individuality, because it holds that each person is unique and irreplaceable. The Father is not the Son, the Son is not the Spirit, and all three of them are essential to God's being as God. On the other hand, these three are, while distinct from one another, not in competition, as in modern indi-vidualism, but entirely for and from one another. There is accordingly an orientation to the other within the eternal structure of God's being.' (Gunton, *Christian Faith*)

Karl Barth, whom Nigel Wright calls 'the outstanding theologian of the early twentieth century with definite opinions on most things,' was so deeply troubled by modern understandings of 'personality' which inevitably imply competition that he went as far as declaring that it was no longer safe to use the term 'person' in reference to the Trinitarian members. God, he said, though three in one, always acts as one and lives in absolute unity without competition or

2.4
Communities that mirror God

If God is a Trinity this brings new depth to what it means to be made in the *imago Dei*. Paul Tillich says, 'The doctrine of the Trinity is the fullest expression of man's relation to God.'[130] The human capacity for relationships (albeit fractured and frail relationships) both with each other and with God is a facet of the image of God.

But more than this, if God is community, a person can never become their true self in isolation, apart from society. Humanity is designed, not only with the capacity, but also the need for community. Genuine personhood is something that we can only enter into by means of relationship with others.

individualism. Because of this, the three persons of the tri-personal God are the only true or whole 'persons'. Human beings become persons only by imitating and participating in God's personhood. We are only ever 'persons' in a secondary sense and in as far as we reflect our Creator.

Life In Community

When Jesus called people to him he brought them into relationship with the Trinity – the community of Father, Son and Holy Spirit.

Jürgen Moltmann, the German theologian, said: 'The loss of the social doctrine of the Trinity has led to the development of possessive individualism within the church and society.'

Individualism is a denial of God's call to community. It's an insufficient view of humanity. Being made in the image of God we are made for community as a call to reflect the nature of God as persons in relationship.

Just as the first disciples were, so we too are called to a radical re-ordering of our lives to embrace community. But living counter culturally and living in community, in whatever expression that finds itself, is no easy thing. There is a famous cartoon depicting the realities of life in a monastic community where one monk has just sunk an axe into the head of another monk. The caption reads 'life in community is never easy!' Community life, sharing your life with others, is always a challenge as well as an opportunity. It exposes inner motives, passions, our hidden attitudes and actions. Commitment to community reveals

the heart like nothing else – but it is a challenge that pushes us onward towards Christlikeness.

In what we call the Sermon on the Mount, Jesus went to the heart of the matter. He called his disciples not to kill, to sleep around or be two-faced. He challenged them to adopt radical principles related to money, sex and power. And this community through which the good news of the gospel was proclaimed and lived would by God's grace impact the world as salt and light and be a blessing to the nations.

With the death throes of Western modernity being felt across our society, God is recalling and reshaping his church to embrace and live out the call to prophetic community – finding a way for living that reflects the nature of God and reveals his purposes in a changing world.

'The renewal of the church will come from a new type of monasticism, which has only in common with the old an uncompromising allegiance to the Sermon on the Mount. It is high time men and women banded together to do this.' (Dietrich Bonhoeffer)

Roy Searle
Leader of the Northumbria Community

However, it wasn't loneliness that prompted God to create the universe. God, because he is Trinity, cannot be lonely. He is three persons in perfect relationship and communication. Rather, it was the perfection of this tri-personal love and interdependence that inspired creation – the desire to share his relationship.

For that reason, Leonardo Boff writes: 'Human society is a pointer on the road to the mystery of the Trinity, while the mystery of the Trinity, as we know it from revelation, is a pointer toward [human] social life.'[131]

As Mother Teresa once observed, loneliness is one of the

Two Popular Errors

As the early church struggled to understand how the Father, Son and Spirit related, the debate inevitably threw up ideas that under examination proved to be misguided and were therefore rejected. However, looking at these is valuable in itself as exploring their implications helps us understand exactly why the idea of the Trinity developed as it did.

Arianism was the belief that Jesus (along with the Holy Spirit) was not eternally pre-existent (i.e. there was a distant time when he did not exist) and that he was created by God. Arius, the architect of this belief, wrote: 'The Son has an origin, but God is unoriginated.' Arius also held that because God was Jesus' creator, and Jesus was his creature, the two were not the same substance – Jesus was not God in the same way that the Father was God. Therefore, there was not equality between God and Jesus.

Elements of Arianism are still very popular today and can be seen in *The Da Vinci Code*, unitarianism, mormonism etc. The next time a Jehovah's Witness calls at your door, talk to them about the first verses of John's Gospel. Their translation reads 'In the beginning was the Word, and the Word was with God, and the Word was a God.' Why? Like Arians they too believe that God created Jesus and so he, the Word of God, was a lesser form of deity.

There are several theological problems with Arianism:

1. If Jesus didn't always exist, then the God we know as Father was not always a father.

2. If Jesus (and the Spirit) didn't always exist, then the God who is love was not always love (see 2.3.1 'God is love').

3. If God has not always been a father and has not always been love he is not unchanging.

4. If God created Jesus, then Jesus was not God and would have no power to repair our broken relationship with God.

5. If Jesus is just a creature (albeit a much older and more magnificent creature than us) we have no place worshipping him as worship is for God alone (Exod 20:3).

Sabellianism (also known as **Modalism**). Sabellius, a third-century Libyan priest living in Rome, claimed there is only one person in the Godhead. The Father, the Son, and the Holy Spirit are all one person with different 'offices', rather than three persons who are one being in the Godhead. Modalism is the belief that God is just one person, but relates to us in three different ways or modes, or with three 'masks'. These modes are consecutive and never simultaneous – the Father, the Son, and the Holy Spirit never all exist at the same time, only one after another. Once again elements of modalism are found in modern movements including, among others, the 'United Pentecostal' and 'United Apostolic' churches, who often accuse trinitarians of teaching three gods.

Sabellianism has great theological weaknesses:

1. If God wears different masks, he is changeable.

2. If God is just one, he cannot be love.

3. If God is just one, the God we know as Father is not a father.

4. If God wears masks, how can we know that we have ever come into true relationship with him?

5. If God is just one – it raises questions about the amount of time Jesus devoted to prayer. Was he talking to his 'Father' in a strange schizophrenic conversation, or was he just having a bit of a think?

upon the congregation to come: so this bell calls us all: but how much more me, who am brought so near the door by this sickness ... No man is an island, entire of itself; every man is a piece of the continent, a part of the main ... any man's death diminishes me, because I am involved in mankind; and therefore never send to know for whom the bell tolls; it tolls for thee.'[133]

2.5
Churches that mirror God

Because God is 'tri-personal', Jürgen Moltmann insists, 'the social doctrine of the Trinity' should serve as the 'critical principle' for the church in its pastoral mission and the transformation of the world.[134]

The Trinity is characterised by mutuality and service rather than domination, hierarchy and lordship. In the words of Joseph Ratzinger, now Pope Benedict XVI, this should also be the 'communal shape of the Christian faith.'[135] He goes on to comment that because the triune God is not a private deity, one cannot create a private fellowship with this God. Genuine Christian faith is Trinitarian faith and therefore necessitates throwing yourself into the community of the church. This does not deny that faith is 'a profoundly personal act anchored in the innermost depths of the human self' but points to the fact that whilst, on one hand, it is 'the act of faith [which] incorporates people into the community [of the church]; on the other hand, it is simultaneously sustained by that community.' (Ratzinger, *Auf Christus Schauen*)[136]

Through the Fall human personhood is perverted. We become individualistic and we learn to affirm ourselves over against, and at the expense of, one another and God. Though we are still in the *imago Dei*, this is only in 'a disrupted fashion and as an unfulfilled tendency'. However, the church constitutes the 'body of Christ' with a mission to bring 'deindividualization' and, as a result, true 'personalization.'[137] This is what Jesus meant when he taught that he had come to bring 'abundant life' or 'life to the full'. He came to help us to be *fully human* – to make us whole. It is the church's responsibility to continue the task. To understand what it means to be made in the image of the social God will affect a 'revolution' in the life of any local congregation.

most prevalent and depressing diseases of the Western world. We live in a culture that often feels acutely impersonal and alienating. In 2004, the body of Kenneth Mann was found by police after having lain undiscovered in his home for six years. To the health authority, we can feel like no more than an NHS number; to the Post Office, a postcode; to the Inland Revenue, a National Insurance number etc. 'I am not a number, I am a free man,' was the famous cry of Patrick McGoohan, star of the '60s TV cult series *The Prisoner*. The tragedy is that, in life, it remains the cry of countless millions of people, both young and old, around the villages, towns and cities of the UK and across our planet today.

Besides being a writer, John Donne was dean of St Paul's Cathedral in London. He held a view of society as being rooted in the life of the Trinity, which he once described as a 'holy and whole college.'[132]

It was just before his death in 1631 that Donne penned his famous words: 'All mankind is of one author, and is one volume; when one man dies, one chapter is not torn out of the book, but translated into a better language; and every chapter must be so translated ... As therefore the bell that rings to a sermon, calls not upon the preacher only, but

QUESTION TIME

1. What does 'Trinity' show us about what it means to be a whole person?

2. What difference does a commitment to Trinitarian theology make to the way we organise our churches?

'More than 200 years ago … America declared its independence. Today we all gather here to declare our interdependence. Today we hold this truth to be self-evident: We are all in this together.' These are the words of actor Will Smith addressing the Live8 concerts around the world from Philadelphia. In an age where we esteem independence and individualism, how can we as the church model prophetic interdependence to our culture?

4

3 Teaching Block 3: The Human God: The Forgiving God

3.1 What is the atonement?

The word *atonement* is almost the only theological term of English origin. The verb *atone* means 'to reconcile' or make 'at one'. The meaning of the word is therefore simply 'at-one-ment'. It is often used in the Old Testament but only occurs once in the New Testament (King James Version) in Romans 5:11 where most other versions use the word *reconciliation*.

For Christians, the word *atonement* is primarily used to denote the effect that flows from Christ's death on the cross, which along with the resurrection is seen by all the New Testament writers as the central act of his life.

'The fact that a cross became the Christian symbol, and that Christians stubbornly refused, in spite of the ridicule, to discard it in favour of something less offensive, can have only one explanation. It means that the centrality of the cross originated in the mind of Jesus himself. It was out of loyalty to him that his followers clung so doggedly to this sign.' (John Stott, *The Cross of Christ*)[138]

However, in a secondary sense, it is also true that the term *atonement* speaks of the sacrifice of Christ's entire life, which culminated with his death and resurrection.

Lesslie Newbigin explains the significance of Christ's death on the cross in this way, 'Essentially what happened was that the human race came face to face with its Creator and its response was to seek to destroy him. This utterly crucial and central moment in universal history is the ground on which we are compelled to say that all of us, the good and bad together, are sinners … It is at that point where we are judged and condemned without distinction. The cross cannot be used as a banner for one part of humanity against another. It is the place where we are all, without distinction, unmasked as the enemies of God. But it is also the place where to all, without distinction, there is offered the unlimited kindness and love of God.'[139]

There is no doubt that we are all sinners in need of forgiveness and salvation. Our broken relationships with God and with each other bear depressing testimony to just this.

But as Michael Lloyd puts it in *Café Theology*, 'The doctrine of the Fall shows that we are fallen and therefore need saving. The doctrine of Creation shows that we are essentially good and therefore worth saving. The doctrine of the Incarnation shows that there is one who is both divine and human and is therefore able to save us.'

We are made in the *imago Dei*, but as we have seen that image, though not lost altogether, has been distorted and marred by the Fall – and the relationship with God that goes with it has been broken through our sin.

Having broken the relationship, humankind has a responsibility to repair it – because it is our fault that it is broken! The problem is that we do not have the power in ourselves to fix it. How can we mend our relationship with God when our means of relating to him is broken? It's a tiny bit like trying to let British Telecom know that your phone isn't working, when your only means of contacting them is on the broken telephone. Through the incarnation the triune God acted decisively to undo the damage we had caused. It was man who needed to mend the broken relationship but only God who could mend it. Only Jesus as God and man could do both.

3.2 How does atonement work?

Over the centuries church fathers and theologians have sought to understand exactly how Christ's sacrifice on the cross atones for our sins. How does Christ's work reverse the Fall and bring about the reconciliation of humankind with God? Various theories have emerged. The New Testament concerns itself with the *fact* of the reconciliation itself, rather than the exact mechanism by which it works.

'God was reconciling the world to himself in Christ, not counting men's sins against them.' (2 Cor 5:19)

'For God was pleased to have all his fulness dwell in him, and through him to reconcile to himself all things, whether things on earth or things in heaven, by making peace through his blood, shed on the cross.' (Col 1:19–20)

In taking our sin on himself, the One who should not die dies in our place. And with his death sin and the consequences of all of our sins are dealt with – death is the consequence of sin and Jesus took it. There is no longer a broken relationship between God and us because he took all of the brokenness away.

The New Testament writers refer to the atoning work of the cross in a number of ways:

Substitution 'For Christ died for sins once for all, the righteous for the unrighteous, to bring you to God.' (1 Pet 3:18, see also Isa 53:5–6)

Ransom 'The Son of Man [came] … to give his life as a ransom for many.' (Matt 20:28)

Identification 'I want to know Christ and … the fellowship of sharing in his sufferings.' (Phil 3:10)

Example 'Take up your cross and follow me.' (Matt 16:24)

Representation 'For just as through the disobedience of the one man the many were made sinners, so also through the obedience of the one man the many will be made righteous.' (Rom 5:19)

Various theories have been built around these to try to explain exactly how the atonement actually works. How did Christ actually make 'peace through his blood'?

In a lecture, entitled 'The Authentic Jesus', Lesslie Newbigin suggests that all metaphors to describe the atoning work of the cross are inadequate in the end.

'All of these metaphors, they point us to the reality. They can never wholly comprehend that reality, because that reality is the ultimate crisis of all cosmic history. It is the point at which the ultimate denial of God is met and mastered, finally and forever by the grace of God. But that is a mystery that is too great for any of our minds wholly to comprehend.

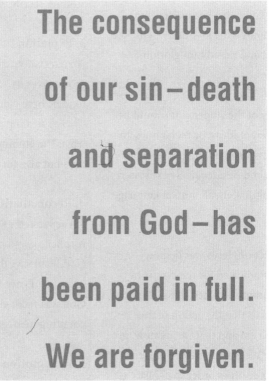

The consequence of our sin – death and separation from God – has been paid in full. We are forgiven.

4

'We can say in all thankfulness that we know that in the cross, God conquered, and we know that because of the resurrection. Because God honoured the love and obedience of his Son, offered on the cross, and raised him glorious from the dead,' Newbigin says.

Any understanding or theology of the atonement should be multifaceted and allow the different ideas, or metaphors, to combine and harmonise to convey something of the depth of a mystery that cannot in the end be adequately expressed by any theory, and for which, ultimately, all human language fails.

As we have seen, in the resurrection, Jesus was demonstrated to be the true Christ – vindicated for the claims he made in his life and of the ignominy attached to his death. Therefore, his resurrection tells us that the action of the cross has successfully dealt with sin and that we are now, in some sense, re-created beings. 'We were therefore buried with him through baptism into death in order that, just as Christ was raised from the dead through the glory of the Father, we too may live a new life.' (Rom 6:4) Through Christ we are no longer sinners separated from God. The consequence of our sin – death and separation from God – has been paid in full. We are forgiven.

What does the atonement mean for us?

The atoning work of Christ has many aspects, and the New Testament uses different words to describe these. The most important of them are:

1. Sacrifice

To pay the price, the penalty of death that we deserved because of our sins, Christ died as a sacrifice for us. 'But now he has appeared once for all at the end of the ages to do away with sin by the sacrifice of himself.' (Heb 9:26)

2. Propitiation

To propitiate means to appease or pacify somebody's anger. Therefore propitiation is to take away the wrath or anger of God that we deserved. Christ died as a propitiation or appeasement for our sins. 'This is love: not that we loved God, but that he loved us and sent his Son as an atoning sacrifice for our sins.' (1 John 4:10)

3. Expiation

An alternative translation of the Greek *hilasterion* word group gives us 'expiation' rather than 'propitiation'. To render these words as expiation places the emphasis on Christ's dealing with sin rather than his appeasing of God. 'He is the atoning sacrifice for our sins, and not only for ours but also for the sins of the whole world.' (1 John 2:2)

4. Reconciliation

Sin separated us from God, and we needed someone to reconcile us, to bring us back into a relationship with God. Paul says that God 'reconciled us to himself through Christ and gave us the ministry of reconciliation: that God was reconciling the world to himself in Christ, not counting men's sins against them.' (2 Cor 5:18–19)

5. Redemption

Sinful humankind is not free, but in bondage or captivity to sin and to Satan. We need someone to redeem us, to pay a ransom, to free us out of that bondage. 'For even the Son of Man did not come to be served, but to serve, and to give his life as a ransom for many.' (Mark 10:45)

3.3
The way of the cross

Augustine taught that from the example of the cross we discover a great truth. The outward sacrifice is always the sacrament (or sign) of the 'invisible sacrifice of the heart'. By his inward sacrifice of obedience to the Father's will, through which he laid down his life for his friends, Christ atoned for our sins and taught us by his example.

'To live under the cross means that every aspect of the Christian community's life is shaped and coloured by it. The cross not only elicits our worship … but it also directs our conduct in relation to others, including our enemies. We are to "be imitators of God … as dearly loved children" and to "live a life of love, just as Christ loved us and gave himself up for us" (Eph 5:1–2).' (Stott, *The Cross*)

In the Sermon on the Mount Jesus teaches us to love our enemies and then suggests that we should pray for those that persecute us.

'But it wasn't just a sermon. As [Christ's] unmistakably compassionate plea from the cross shows – "Father, forgive them, for they know not what they do" – he practised what he preached.'[141]

However, in the same sermon Jesus goes on to urge his followers: 'If you forgive men when they sin against you, your heavenly Father will also forgive you.' Then, having taught his disciples to pray 'Forgive us our debts, as we also have forgiven our debtors', he starkly warns 'but if you do not forgive men their sins, your Father will not forgive your sins.' (Matt 6:14–15)

What do these words actually mean? Jesus unpacks his teaching further in the Parable of the Unmerciful Servant, which is almost a commentary on his earlier words. Is it that the strongest motivation for forgiveness is the sense of having received forgiveness ourselves? Once we recognise our own need of forgiveness will we be able to forgive?

'If only there were evil people somewhere insidiously committing evil deeds, and it were necessary to separate them from the rest of us and destroy them! But the line dividing good from evil cuts through the heart of every human being. And who is willing to destroy a piece of his own heart?' (Aleksandr Solzhenitsyn)[142]

'The cross is the means by which evil is overcome which means that Christ did something once for all that is redemptive; he made atonement. But it means more. The cross sets the pattern for the power of redemption. It is cross-like action, becoming like Christ in his death, that introduces redeeming power into a fallen world. Over all it must be by imitating Christ, by using the weapons of self-giving love and compassion, by identifying with the outcast and the poor rather than the rich and powerful and refusing to continue the vicious cycle of human hostility and aggression that Christian people serve the coming of Christ's kingdom.' (Wright, *Dark Side*)

The church faces a choice between 'the love of power and the power of love.' (Wright, *Dark Side*)

The cross calls us to respond and that involves not merely identifying with Jesus and his suffering but responding to his death in personal repentance and faith.

3.4
Learning to forgive – A personal principle

Clearly real forgiveness has little to do with human fairness, which demands an eye for an eye, or with excusing, which means brushing something aside.

After the end of the Second World War, when the full horrors of the Holocaust had only just come to light, C.S. Lewis wrote: 'There is all the difference in the world between forgiving and excusing … but if one is not really to blame, then there is nothing to forgive. In that sense forgiveness and excusing are almost opposites.'[143]

Arnold says: 'When we forgive someone for a deliberate hurt, we still recognise it as such, but instead of lashing out or biting back, we attempt to see beyond it, so as to restore our relationship with the person responsible for it. Our forgiveness may not take away the pain – it may not even be acknowledged or accepted – yet the act of offering it will keep us from being sucked into the downward spiral of

4.

'There is no way that we can live a rich life unless we are willing to suffer repeatedly, experiencing depression and despair, fear and anxiety, grief and sadness, anger and the agony of forgiveness … A life lacking these emotional upheavals will not only be useless to ourselves; it will be useless to others.' (M. Scott Peck)[146]

3   3.5
Learning to forgive – A global principle

'One of the most pressing questions facing the world today is, How can we oppose evil without creating new evils and being made evil ourselves?' (Walter Wink)[147]

Far from leaving us weak, forgiveness is empowering both to the giver and the receiver – it allows them to lay aside the riddles of retribution and human fairness and to experience true peace.

resentment. It will also guard us from the danger of taking out our anger or resentment on someone else.'[144]

Forgiving does not mean forgetting or condoning wrong. But it does require initiative and courage from the person who has been wronged. Martin Luther King says: 'It is … necessary to realise that the forgiving act must always be initiated by the person who has been wronged, the victim of some great hurt, the recipient of some tortuous injustice, the absorber of some terrible act of oppression … Forgiveness does not mean ignoring what has been done or putting a false label on an evil act. It means, rather, that the evil act no longer remains a barrier to the relationship…'[145]

Bitterness is a destructive and self-destructive power. It feeds on every new thought of spite or hatred. And like an ulcer aggravated by worry, it can be physically as well as emotionally debilitating. We all know people who defend their grudges. People who feel they have been hurt too deeply and too often, and that this exempts them from the need to forgive. However, we also know that it is just these people who need to forgive most of all. 'There is a hard law … When an injury is done to us, we never recover until we forgive.' (Arnold, *Why*)

But forgiveness is not an occasional act – it is a permanent attitude.

Though often misunderstood, this principle based on Jesus' teaching has been embraced by hundreds of persecuted minorities throughout history from the earliest Christians, to the Anabaptists, to followers of Tolstoy, Gandhi, Martin Luther King and the black churches in South Africa. These groups have all believed that forgiveness, however difficult, is the only way to break the cycle of vengeance and reprisal which, once installed within a community, otherwise becomes self-perpetuating. King's commitment to love and forgiveness as political weapons grew directly out of his understanding of Christ's teaching and example.

'Probably no admonition of Jesus has been more difficult to follow than the command to love your enemies. Some people have sincerely felt that its actual practice is not possible. It is easy, they say, to love those who love you, but how can one love those who openly and insidiously seek to defeat you … ?

'Far from being the pious injunction of a Utopian dreamer, the command to love one's enemy is an absolute necessity for our survival. Love even our enemies is the key to the solution of the problems of our world. Jesus is not the impractical idealist; he is the practical realist … Returning hate for hate multiplies hate … Darkness cannot drive out darkness; only the light can do that … Hate multiplies hate, violence multiplies violence, and toughness multiplies toughness in a descending spiral of destruction … Love is the only force capable of transforming an enemy into a friend … Love transforms with redemptive power.' (King, *Strength*)

American author Jim Wallis has pointed out that Jesus' words 'Love your enemies'[148] probably amount to, at one and the same time, 'the most admired and least practised piece of teaching in history'. More often than not, Jesus' advice is viewed as impractical idealism, though, extraordinarily, no such charge is ever made against violence, in spite of the fact that history has proved, time and again, revenge solves nothing in the long run.

Our God is the Human God.

A few months after 11 September 2001, a well-known American leader was interviewed on national television. It was Christmas morning, so he began by reminding his interviewer and audience: 'Christmas is about peace and goodwill to all … Jesus is the Prince of Peace – we must never close ourselves to his message.'

'So if Jesus is the Prince of Peace and one of his key messages was love your enemies, what does that mean on a world scale?' the interviewer asked. 'How should it affect American foreign policy? What is your message to world leaders this Christmas?'

His reply was short, 'I think it's easier to understand Jesus' message on a person-to-person level – it doesn't necessarily apply to nation/state relationships.'

One God: The Human God

4.

QUESTION TIME

1. Naim Ateek, a church leader in Jerusalem, writes:

'When people hate, its power engulfs them and they are totally consumed by it … Never stop trying to live the commandment of love and forgiveness. Do not dilute the strength of Jesus' message; do not shun it; do not dismiss it as unreal and impractical. Do not cut it to your size, trying to make it more applicable to real life in the world. Do not change it so that it will suit you. Keep it as it is, aspire to it, desire it, and work for its achievement.'[149]

In the volatile situations we face today can we trust the same principle? Why? Are there problems with it?

2. Think of a situation you are in where there is conflict. What do you need to do to bring peace?

3. Reflect on the words of the Peace Prayer of Saint Francis. What does it mean for you?

Make me a channel of your peace.
Where there is hatred let me bring your love.
Where there is injury, your pardon, Lord
And where there's doubt, true faith in you.

Oh, Master grant that I may never seek
So much to be consoled as to console
To be understood as to understand
To be loved as to love with all my soul.

Make me a channel of your peace
Where there's despair in life, let me bring hope
Where there is darkness, only light
And where there's sadness, ever joy.

Make me a channel of your peace
It is in pardoning that we are pardoned
In giving to all men that we receive
And in dying that we're born to eternal life.

FURTHER READING

The Challenge of Jesus by N.T. Wright (SPCK, 2000) is an engaging study of Jesus as a historical figure that goes on to consider what our response to him should be today.

The Bible Speaks Today: The Message of the Cross by Derek Tidball (IVP, 2001) is a comprehensive guide to the significance of Jesus' death on the cross from the Old Testament to today.

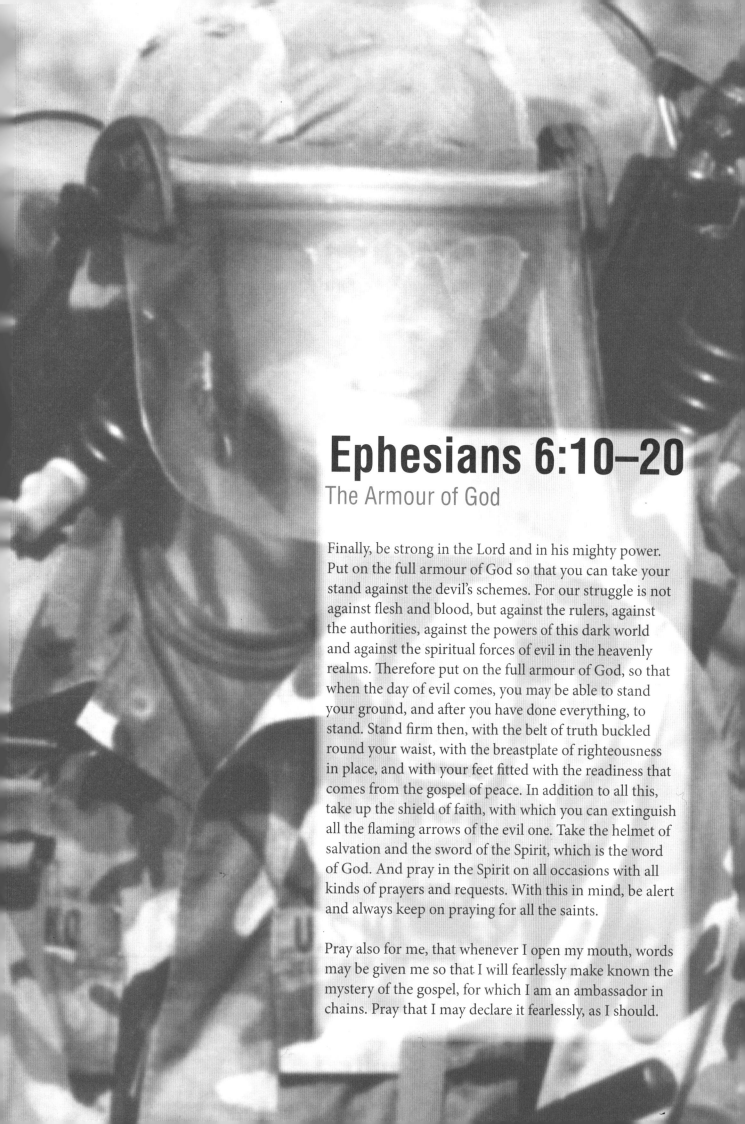

Ephesians 6:10–20
The Armour of God

Finally, be strong in the Lord and in his mighty power. Put on the full armour of God so that you can take your stand against the devil's schemes. For our struggle is not against flesh and blood, but against the rulers, against the authorities, against the powers of this dark world and against the spiritual forces of evil in the heavenly realms. Therefore put on the full armour of God, so that when the day of evil comes, you may be able to stand your ground, and after you have done everything, to stand. Stand firm then, with the belt of truth buckled round your waist, with the breastplate of righteousness in place, and with your feet fitted with the readiness that comes from the gospel of peace. In addition to all this, take up the shield of faith, with which you can extinguish all the flaming arrows of the evil one. Take the helmet of salvation and the sword of the Spirit, which is the word of God. And pray in the Spirit on all occasions with all kinds of prayers and requests. With this in mind, be alert and always keep on praying for all the saints.

Pray also for me, that whenever I open my mouth, words may be given me so that I will fearlessly make known the mystery of the gospel, for which I am an ambassador in chains. Pray that I may declare it fearlessly, as I should.

5

The BIG ISSUE

Teaching Block 1

The Sovereign God: The Problem of Evil

1.1 Why do we suffer?

1.2 Moral evil

1.3 Natural evil

1.4 The gift of pain

1.5 Natural evil is the result of humanity's fall

1.6 Natural evil is the result of the devil's fall

QUESTION TIME

Teaching Block 2

The Sovereign God: When Pain is Personal

2.1 A grief observed

2.2 The vulnerable God

2.3 The suffering servant

2.4 Christ as inspiration

QUESTION TIME

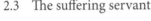

Teaching Block 3

The Sovereign God: The Ongoing Battle

3.1 God at war

3.2 Know your enemy

3.3 What is your worldview?

3.4 The power of prayer

QUESTION TIME

FURTHER READING

THE BIG STORY
ONE GOD 1
Celebrating the one true God

The BIG ISSUE

'If God is so loving, and he knows all about our suffering, why doesn't he do something about it?'

'A loving and all powerful God would never allow people to suffer as they do.'

These age-old complaints put God fairly and squarely in the dock – accused of negligence, impotence or just a lack of compassion.

For centuries, Christians have argued in God's defence. And yet still, every day, the cry goes up around the world: 'How can a loving God allow this to go on?'

The nuclear devastation of Hiroshima and Nagasaki, the Nazi death camps, the murder of innocent and helpless children, the piloting of aircraft into the World Trade Centre, the genocides of Rwanda, Bosnia and Iraq, the suffering of the ordinary people of Zimbabwe – it's all so overwhelming. In fact, increasing numbers of people even excuse themselves from believing in God altogether on the basis that they have 'seen too much' in life. For them a simple hopeful belief in a loving God seems utterly naïve in the face of our cruel world.

In his book *Night*, Elie Wiesel, a Hungarian Jew, describes his reaction to his first night in the Nazi camp of Birkenau, the 'reception centre' for Auschwitz. Here the fifteen-year-old Wiesel, whose passion for God had been his whole life, saw his faith evaporate.

'Never shall I forget that night, the first night in the camp, which has turned my life into one long night, seven times cursed and seven times sealed. Never shall I forget that smoke. Never shall I forget the little faces of the children, whose bodies I saw turned into wreaths of smoke beneath a silent blue sky. Never shall I forget those flames which consumed my faith forever. Never shall I forget that nocturnal silence, which deprived me, for all eternity, of the desire to live. Never shall I forget those moments which murdered my God and my soul and turned my dreams to dust.'[150]

Wiesel, who once spent his evenings eagerly studying the Jewish holy writings, found himself unable even to join in with prayers for the Jewish New Year.

'This day I had ceased to plead,' he writes. 'I was no longer capable [even] of lamentation. On the contrary, I felt very strong. I was the accuser, God the accused … I did not deny God's existence, but I doubted his absolute justice.'

Wiesel's complaint is a common one, although not everyone who voices it has been through so horrific an ordeal as a Nazi death camp. The existence of suffering and evil in the world are seen as incompatible with the Jewish and Christian belief in an all-powerful and loving God. Surely if God really cared about people who were suffering he would do something to help? He would end their suffering. Yet people continue to suffer.

- How can anyone believe in a just, benevolent and omnipotent God in the face of the world as we know it?
- If God is God why does he appear to abandon us, so often, just when we need him most?
- If Christ won such a great victory over evil – why is poverty, disease and suffering still so widespread?

5

Teaching Block 1: The Sovereign God: The Problem of Evil

1.1
Why do we suffer?

When we say that our God is the one true, sovereign God – all knowing (omniscient), constantly and universally available (omnipresent) and all powerful (omnipotent) – a significant question looms large. Why do bad things happen? This issue has vexed humanity throughout history and has filled the pages of countless books of theology and philosophy.

'As you sow, so shall you reap' was the prevailing theory at the time when the book of Job was written. God punishes people for the wrong they have done to him and to others, or for their lack of faith. When Job's wealth is taken from him, his children killed and his body covered in sores, he is visited by three friends. They are so shocked by what has happened to him that none of them speaks for a whole week. But when they do finally start talking, it's to tell Job (in as kind and gentle a way as they can) that it was all his fault and he should repent of his sin!

Then God will forgive him and restore his health and for-tune: 'But if you look to God and plead with the Almighty, if you are pure and upright, even now he will rouse himself on your behalf and restore you to your rightful place.' (Job 8:5–6)

As his friends become more and more convinced of his guilt, Job becomes equally convinced of his innocence. He begins to question God's justice. However, though he knows that he is suffering unjustly, even he can't quite shake off the belief that people suffer only for their sins. Therefore, Job cannot understand what is happening – God has got it wrong.

The breakthrough comes when Job finally looks beyond himself and his own suffering to see the suffering of others. It occurs to him that if he is suffering even though he is innocent, other innocent people must be suffering as well. He comes to understand that it's not God's morality, or even his own, which is at fault. It's his theology. He finally lets go of the idea that people only suffer as punishment for their sins. Then the Lord God himself answers Job out of the storm, and his questions are stilled.

He still doesn't understand why people suffer, and comes to accept that he may never understand: 'Surely I spoke of things I did not understand, things too wonderful for me to know.' (Job 42:3)

Job has changed. Seeing God has changed him: 'My ears had heard of you, but now my eyes have seen you.' (42:5) He now knows God (and himself) in a new way and all else, his days of suffering and of plenty, pales in comparison.

'We must firmly repudiate the … dreadful doctrine of Job's so-called comforters. They trotted out their conventional orthodoxy that all personal suffering is due to personal sin, and one of the major purposes of the book of Job is to contradict that popular but wrong-headed notion.' (John Stott)[151]

Of course, people do suffer because of their sins. Not as a punishment, but as a consequence. Picture this: a man is walking along a beautiful but deserted beach in the middle of which is a sign saying: 'Shark Infested Waters: No Swimming.' The sea is warm and inviting, so he ignores the advice. His subsequent death is not a punishment for his stupidity, but simply the natural consequence of it!

However, the difficulties with an 'all evil is a punishment for sin' view of life include the facts that:

- Evil is a crude instrument of retribution; it often smites hardest those who have sinned least.
- It fails to explain the unequal distribution of natural evil that we observe around the world.
- When Jesus heals the man born blind, he states clearly that his blindness was not due to sin: 'Neither this man nor his parents sinned,' said Jesus, 'but this happened so that the work of God might be displayed in his life.' (John 9:3)
- The fallacy of the idea that people suffer only for the sins they themselves have committed is nowhere seen more clearly for the Christian than in the death of Jesus, who was totally without sin.

It was the German philosopher Gottfried Wilhelm von Leibniz (1646–1716) who first made a distinction between the forms of evil that we see in our world. He said that people suffer both as a result of 'moral evil' and 'physical evil' (usually known today as 'natural evil'). The two pose different questions and demand different responses.

1.2
Moral evil

Moral evil refers to evil that can be directly attributed to the human race – atrocities from the heinous crimes of Nazi Germany to the multiple murders of Dr Harold Shipman (who killed an estimated 260 of his patients). Moral evil does not, however, solely refer to the great crimes of our world – ethnic cleansing, murder, persecution, poverty and injustice. It also includes all the smaller, common-or-garden, everyday acts of selfishness – deceit, theft, rejection, misrepresentation, abuse, exploitation – that cause others pain.

Though moral evil causes huge problems for us emotionally, it poses few at a logical or intellectual level. We understand that many bad things happen because people choose to sin and sin brings consequences into our world. This is technically known as 'the free-will defence'. It holds two principles to be true.

If God is love, why does he not intervene to stop malicious or negligent human action that will inevitably cause pain and suffering?

Moral evil is caused by the choices of 'free moral agents'

Put bluntly, moral evil is not God's fault; it is ours. The tragedy is that the consequences of those wrong choices often, indeed normally, engulf innocent people – both in ways that we experience every day and also in world events like the terrorist bombings in countries such as Israel, Iraq, Bali, Kenya, Spain and the United Kingdom.

In 1877, the Russian novelist Fyodor Dostoevsky wrote a short story called *The Dream of A Ridiculous Man*. In it he attacked what he saw as false optimism about human nature. A man on the brink of suicide dreams of flying to another planet millions of miles away – a planet that is identical to the earth except that everyone there is innocent and happy. They know no sin or evil, and no suffering. The man is overawed by their beauty and their love.

5

'terrorism') as the 'focus of evil in the modern world' then it makes it easier to decide what I must do. If as in Nazi Germany, the ills of society can be blamed upon the Jews, then life's complex decisions become much easier, since someone else is to blame and not me.' (Nigel Wright)[153]

G.K. Chesterton sought to combat this thinking in his now famous letter to *The Times*. The newspaper had asked its readers, 'What's wrong with the world?' Over the course of a few months all sorts of people wrote in suggesting answers. Chesterton's contribution was essentially just two words long:

> 'Dear Sir, "I am."
> Yours sincerely,
> G.K. Chesterton.'

'But now,' he recalls when his dream is over, 'I will tell you the whole truth. The fact is I corrupted them all! … Like the germ of the plague infecting whole kingdoms, so did I infect with myself all that happy earth that knew no sin before me. They learnt to lie, and they grew to appreciate the beauty of a lie. Oh, perhaps, it all began innocently, with a jest, with a desire to show off, with amorous play, and perhaps indeed only with a germ, but this germ made its way into their hearts and they liked it.'[152]

As Paul told the church in Rome, 'All have sinned and fall short of the glory of God.' (Rom 3:23)

Thus, the question posed by moral evil is simply this: 'Why does God allow us to act in ways that harm ourselves and others around us?'

In Dostoevsky's tale, the minor sins of one man were enough to corrupt an entire world, and over the course of thousands of years to make it just as bad as the one he had left.

If God is love, why does he not intervene to stop malicious or negligent human action that will inevitably cause pain and suffering to ourselves and others?

The Bible tells a similar story in Noah's ark (Gen 6 – 9). Appalled by the amount and cruelty of people's sin, God instructs Noah, the only man he is prepared to call 'blameless' (Gen 6:9), to build a boat and to fill it with his family and a variety of animals. God will wipe the slate clean, destroying everyone else. Yet this fresh start is a false start, for no sooner has Noah got off the boat after the flood than he and his sons fall back into sin. Noah was a good man, yet even he was not upright enough to stop sin from creeping back into the world.

It is more important that 'free moral agents' do exist than that moral evil does not exist

The argument that God cannot be both omnipotent and loving is an over-simplification. God is all-powerful but that does not mean he can do things which are logically impossible (eg create a square circle!). In our creation, God granted us the gift of freedom – but this great gift comes at a price. It is logically impossible for God to create free beings – rather than robots – who automatically do what is right. We are therefore free to disobey God and hurt others if we choose.

'The world is a far simpler place if we identify the enemy and project all our fears and doubts on to him, it, her or them. If I can attribute the rot in my society to the subversive influence (say) of communist infiltrators then I have some sort of framework for living and acting in the world. If I am able to identify agents (it used to be the Soviets but it is now more likely to be nations sponsoring

'If you choose to say "God can give a creature free will and at the same time withhold free will from it", you have not succeeded in saying anything about God: meaningless combinations of words do not suddenly acquire meaning simply because we prefix to them the two other words "God can". It remains true that all things are possible with God [but] … nonsense remains nonsense even when we talk it about God,' C.S. Lewis explains.[154]

God, Freedom, and Human Responsibility

'The greatest gift that God in his bounty made in creation, the most conformable to his goodness and that which he prizes the most was freedom of will.' So wrote Dante Alighieri in *The Divine Comedy*. His words are worthy of careful analysis since they so well encapsulate the deepest meanings of God-centred freedom.

A believer starts from the premise that freedom is not merely a gift from God but the greatest of his gifts. All other gifts (beauty, strength, courage, talent, etc. – the list is endless) are important but free will is supremely so. For it is a universal gift to all humankind, bringing with it the freedom of choice. And the hardest choice we all have to face is: Do we or do we not use our free will to make ourselves 'conformable to his goodness?' Most of us fail to exercise our freedom in a way that is pleasing to God and conformable to his will - for human freedom and divine freedom are so often in conflict.

During my two years of reading theology at Wycliffe Hall, Oxford, I sometimes used to think that concepts such as original sin, the theology of grace and its conflict with free will were unbearably complicated. But they became clearer when I applied them to my own personal and spiritual journey.

There have been times in my life when I have used my free will to commit deliberate acts of sin – most notoriously telling a lie on oath. But alas, there were many comparable, and probably worse, deliberate rebellions against the divine will.

Much more of the time I was in a largely unthinking state of sin, a distorted relationship with God. I call this my Sunday Christian phase. I was at best a half Christian which I now know is about as much use as being half pregnant. For what God wants is total conformity to his will, and complete obedience to his divine sovereignty. To head in this direction requires the complete commitment of our human free will. That is the path towards the gift of God's grace which is generously given to those who turn to him in penitence and faith.

Seven years ago I found this path, and pray daily not to stray from it. Everyone has the freedom to search for the same path but it requires a massive commitment of human responsibility to seek and find the ultimate goal which St Paul summarised with the words: 'You were called to freedom, brothers. The freedom for which Christ has set us free.' (Gal 5:13)

Jonathan Aitken
former Conservative MP and cabinet minister

'The permanent nature of wood which enables us to use it as a beam also enables us to use it for hitting our neighbour on the head … We can, perhaps, conceive of a world in which God corrected the results of this abuse of free will by his creatures at every moment: so that a wooden beam became soft as grass when it was used as a weapon … [however] if the principle were carried out to its logical conclusion, evil thoughts would be impossible, for the cerebral matter which we use in thinking would refuse its task when we attempted to frame them … Try to exclude the possibility of suffering which the order of nature and the existence of free wills involve, and you find that you have excluded life itself.'

By endowing us with freedom, God imposed certain restrictions on himself. If his children were to be free, they must do his will by voluntary choice. God cannot impose his will upon humanity and also maintain his purpose for us. Therefore, the fact of evil in the world does not so much represent a weakness in God's love for us, but instead is clear evidence of its abundance – a less loving Creator would not have granted us freedom with all of the 'glories' and 'tragedies' that go hand in hand with it.

1.3
Natural evil

Unlike moral evil, natural evil refers to events and problems that cannot be attributed in any direct sense to the moral choices of humans, eg a painful death resulting from an

5

It was All Saints' Day, 1 November 1755. An event was about to take place that would rock the faith of Christian Europe and challenge their way of thinking about evil. At 9.30am a massive earthquake devastated Lisbon, the capital of Portugal. Three tremors in the space of ten minutes left 15,000 people dead and another 15,000 dying. Because it was All Saints' Day, huge numbers of those who died did so precisely because they were in packed church buildings (thirty of which were completely destroyed) attending services. What shocked people was that the majority of those who survived were those who had no faith and, therefore, were not 'in church' that morning. The popular view, held by the majority of people at the time, was still that all evil came on you as the result of sin and that God particularly protected the faithful. But as news of the disaster spread round Europe this belief was shattered. For the first time, on a mass scale, ordinary people began to ask themselves the question, 'Was God really the loving and faithful Father that the church taught him to be?'

In the wake of the Lisbon earthquake Voltaire, the French philosopher and writer, published *Poème sur le désastre de Lisbonne* (Poem on the Lisbon Disaster). In it he mocked the idea that everything that happens in the world is for the best. For him, the idea that all those who died in Lisbon were sinners who were justly the victims of God's anger was absurd. How could anyone now believe in a just, benevolent and omnipotent God? He ridiculed the claim that disasters were, in some sense, God judging, testing or improving us.

Where was God when the South Asian tsunami struck?

I was on holiday in India in December 2004 when, on Boxing Day, a massive offshore earthquake caused an enormous tsunami to engulf much of the coast of Southeast Asia – about 280,000 died and there is still tremendous devastation in lives and livelihoods across the Indian Ocean. Christian Aid also works in Africa where similar death rates are clocked up every 10 days without ever reaching the news. A child dies from poverty and preventable causes every 3 seconds. Where is God in all this?

It would be trite to suggest that some good comes out of every situation – the tsunami was nothing other than a terrible disaster. However, even in the midst of those first terrible days in India I saw local people responding across castes and communities – standing together in ways that they would never normally do. Further afield the Western world was, in some sense, united with the East as millions of people gave sacrificially to our joint Tsunami Appeal.

I cannot believe God plays with our individual lives and chose 26 December 2005 to shatter the dreams of millions in the Asian region. But I do believe that he is there in all situations – in our pain and suffering as well as our joys and success. God was there in the tsunami, and in some way suffering with us as he worked with his people to bring meaning out of chaos.

This strengthens my faith. Months on, I still struggle with the question 'why Lord?', and yet I believe I saw God working in and through the response of millions – locally, internationally and globally. I pray regularly for God's kingdom to come – and even in the pain and horror of the tsunami, I believe I saw small signs of hope for a better world.

Dr Daleep Mukarji
Executive Director, Christian Aid

ONE GOD 1
Celebrating the one true God

incurable terminal disease or the suffering caused by natural disasters such as earthquakes, hurricanes, floods, volcanic eruptions, forest fires, droughts, lightning strikes and tsunamis.

It is significant that these catastrophic events are frequently referred to as 'acts of God' simply because of the belief that if the blame for them cannot be laid at humanity's door, God must be culpable! The existence of natural evil poses serious questions about God's nature calling some to conclude that if the creation reflects the character of its Creator, then surely he must have his cruel and dark side too.

In 1874, John Stuart Mill, a leading English philosopher of the nineteenth century, published *Nature and Utility of Religion*. In it he argued that any reasonable look at the world suggests that there is no God in control. Nature is reckless, cruel and indifferent to life – diseases like cholera, malaria and typhoid daily wipe out countless innocent people. Only the most distorted view could lead one to suppose that the world was governed by a good and all-powerful God:

'In sober truth, nearly all the things which men are hanged or imprisoned for doing to one another are nature's every-day performances. Killing, the most criminal act recognized by human laws, nature does once to every being that lives, and in a large proportion of cases after protracted tortures such as only the greatest monsters whom we read of ever purposely inflicted on their living fellow creatures.'[155]

In our own day, it is just as difficult to reconcile the concept of a sovereign and loving God with the fact of the massive earthquake that generated the Southeast Asian tsunami killing over 280,000 people on the 26 December 2004. Why didn't he intervene? As a letter to one broadsheet newspaper expressed it during the following week: *'The world has found itself united in a single prayer "How could you let this happen?" Either God caused the wave to form, in which case he is malevolent, or he failed to act to stop it, in which case he is negligent.'*

Based on the teaching of the Bible, Christians are convinced that:

God is good – 'Taste and see that the Lord is good; blessed is the man who takes refuge in him.' (Ps 34:8)

God is all powerful – 'I am the Alpha and the Omega,' says the Lord God, 'who is, and who was, and who is to come, the Almighty.' (Rev 1:8)

Because of this, Christians have sought to shed light on the question of natural evil in a number of other ways.

1.4
The gift of pain

Although suffering and evil are very real, they are part of a bigger picture. They are awful when we are close to them because we can't get a true perspective on them. If we had

In his book *Where is God When it Hurts*, Philip Yancey highlights the importance of the body's ability to feel physical pain. The pain sensors of the central nervous system give valuable warning signals, necessary for personal survival.

'The pain network is easily the most unappreciated bodily system. It attracts mostly abuse and bad feelings … Pain is usually defined as "unpleasantness." Christians, who believe in a loving Creator, don't really know how to interpret pain. If pinned against the wall at a dark, secret moment, many Christians would confess that pain was God's one mistake … However, I am convinced that pain gets a bad press… because up close, under a microscope, the pain network … bears the marks of creative genius.'[156]

C.S. Lewis further explains how our attitude to pain depends largely on the circumstances.

'If fire comforts [the] body at a certain distance, it will destroy it when the distance is reduced. Hence, even in a perfect world, the necessity for those danger signals which the pain-fibres in our nerves are apparently designed to transmit … Does this mean an inevitable element of evil (in the form of pain) in any possible world? I think not … No-one minds the process 'warm – beautifully hot – too hot – it stings' which warns him to withdraw his hand from exposure to the fire: and if I may trust my own feeling, a slight aching in the legs as we climb into bed after a good day's walking is, in fact, pleasurable.'[157]

makes us feel bad or causes us discomfort, we assume it is 'bad'. Likewise, if something pleases us or brings us happiness, we assume it is good. We project our short-range, personal, and experiential definitions of good onto God. But this is not an adequate basis to make these sorts of judgments.

Of course, there is some truth in all this. The value of pain as a gift is certainly something to think about next time you touch a hot plate or stove – were it not for the unpleasant sensation you feel, who knows what damage you might do to yourself. As the author of Hebrews explains, suffering can be a discipline.

'No discipline seems pleasant at the time, but painful. Later on, however, it produces a harvest of righteousness and peace for those who have been trained by it.' (Heb 12:11)

And as Paul says, 'In all things God works for the good of those who love him.' (Rom 8:28) He also uses (v22) the imagery of pregnancy, suggesting the hope that our pains will be followed by blessings. Many people who have undergone intense suffering would agree – they've grown as a result and have learned valuable lessons from it.

the power of hindsight then we would realise that suffering is like the darker squares in a patchwork quilt. God allows us to suffer so that we might grow from the experience. Looking back we may say we have benefited from many unpleasant and difficult circumstances and that we are better people as a result:

> ## The fact that God can and does bring good out of evil does not mean that evil is 'good'.

- When a couple's young daughter dies from leukaemia, it seems like a tragedy. But when it brings the rest of the family closer together, prompting them to resolve conflicts and hatred which have festered like a wound for many years, threatening to break the family apart completely, it begins to seem more positive.

- A successful businessman is struck down with multiple sclerosis. But as a result, he learns to stop and smell the roses. He sorts through his priorities to discover what really matters in life. Two years later, his wife says that their marriage is stronger than it's ever been in the past.

The problem is not really with God but with our assumptions about what God ought to be. Though we say that God is good, we tend to define 'good' and 'bad' in relation to ourselves and from a short-range perspective. If something

However, as Nigel Wright writes in *The Theology of the Dark Side*, 'The difficulty comes in accounting for the forms of pain that cannot be made to fit into this scheme and are seemingly without meaning.'

What about the times when no good at all seems to come from suffering? When there *is* no 'happy ever after'? What if, rather than bringing their extended family closer together, the death of a couple's daughter caused *more* division and hurt within the family? What if, unable to cope with the differences in how each came to terms with their loss, the couple grew apart, ending their marriage in divorce?

'I know of no other Christian leader who has been more

forthright in confessing his anger [at God] than Joseph Parker, who was the minister of City Temple from 1874 until his death in 1902. He says in his autobiography that up to the age of 68 he never had a religious doubt. Then his wife died, and his faith collapsed. 'In that dark hour', he wrote, 'I became an atheist. For God had set his foot upon my prayers and treated petitions with contempt. If I had seen a dog in such agony … I would have pitied and helped the dumb beast; yet God spat upon me and cast me out as an offence,' Wright says.[158]

What about the many people who suffer out of all reasonable proportion to the lessons they are able to learn from it? There are forms of pain for which we can offer no real explanation; for instance, the onset of even the most aggressive cancer is not usually accompanied by pain as a 'warning' that something is wrong. Instead, the process is the other way round – the cancer begins painlessly and only when it has already taken hold becomes progressively more painful until it is unbearable – even leading people to want to take their own lives. The Hospice Movement was founded to provide relief from such pain, which seems to serve no useful purpose.

The fact that God can and does bring good out of evil does not mean that evil is 'good'. How can the death of a child, a friend dying of cancer, or a tornado that devastates thousands of homes in a few minutes be inherently good? To begin to believe this is to move into the absurd. If we somehow declare that evil is no longer truly evil; if we lose sight of the idea of the ultimate hostility between God and evil, we are in danger of turning the Trinity into what Nigel Wright calls a 'Quaternity' in which Satan takes his place along with the Father, Son and Holy Spirit.[159]

Whatever good can come from suffering in the long run is the result of God and human beings rescuing victory from the jaws of defeat. It doesn't make the suffering any less real. It just stops it from being the end of the story.

1.5
Natural evil is the result of humanity's fall

This view denies that any evil is truly 'natural'. According to John Calvin sin 'perverted the whole order of nature in heaven and on earth.'[160] All conflict, cruelty, pain and death

in creation is therefore attributed, directly or indirectly, to the Fall. Genesis 1 – 3 clearly portrays creation as 'good' and the rebellion of humankind as the point at which it became corrupted. It was the free decision of the first man that brought death into our world.

In Romans 5:12, Paul tells us that sin and death entered the world through Adam: 'Therefore, just as sin entered the world through one man, and death through sin, and in this way death came to all men, because all sinned'. And later in Romans 8:20–21 he goes on to explain that the whole creation is therefore 'subjected to frustration', but 'waits in eager expectation' for one day it too 'will be liberated from its bondage to decay'.

Natural evil is, therefore, attributed to humankind – and God is cleared of responsibility for it. The Fall of the human race has led to the Fall of the whole creation. The natural evil we see does not properly belong to creation but is there simply because of the Fall of humankind.

However, while it is beyond doubt that humans have a negative impact on the environment (eg the selfish exploitation of the planet), and while it is also true that some disease is directly linked with our choices and behaviours once again there are a number of problems with this view.

A world without death and decay would be radically different from the world we know.

'Indeed, Genesis [1-3] does not suggest a world [prior to humanity's Fall] that is perfect and not prone to decay. Adam and Eve are placed in the Garden to subdue and to manage it, presumably because it had the capacity to get out of hand.'[161]

Humankind is given the role of 'subduing' the earth in the sense that there is disorder to be overcome. The presence of 'the serpent' within the 'pre-Fall' world of Adam and Eve acts as further evidence of the view that all was not perfect prior to humanity's rebellion against God.

'Here we have an indication that human sin, potent though it may be, nevertheless needs to be understood within the wider context of a power working in opposition to God,' Wright says.

5

He further argues that the death that enters the world through sin is 'not physical cessation of existence but the death of alienation and anxiety that is characteristic of humanity out of fellowship with God.' It is the spiritual death which, in due course, results in the fear, isolation and loneliness of physical death alienated from God.

For those who do not take a literal view of the six days of creation, evidence of death as well as pain within the animal kingdom before the emergence of humankind on earth is unambiguously contained in the fossil records.

Some who hold to the view that all natural evil is the result of moral evil, but understand that all was not perfect before the Fall of humanity, argue that moral evil not only affected the Fall of the physical universe *prospectively* (in terms of the future) but also *retrospectively* (i.e. before the actual time of Adam's sin, due to God's foreknowledge). So Bruce Milne[162] states: 'All our sinning flows from Adam's primal act of folly which subjected the whole universe prospectively and retrospectively to the forces of decay and cosmic wickedness, and hence to the possibility of suffering and tragedy.'

1.6
Natural evil is the result of the devil's fall

According to this view, natural evils – earthquakes, epidemics, etc. – are the work of demonic forces or fallen angels so when we refer to natural evils as 'acts of God' we misname them. The fall of angels is understood to be a rebellion against God by spiritual beings that he created, which took place before the Fall of humankind. The early church fathers – including Origen, Tertullian and Augustine – all taught this on the basis of their understanding of Ezekiel 28:1–17 and Isaiah 14:12–21, as well as Jude 6 and 2 Peter 2:4.

'If this is accepted it becomes possible to think in terms of physical evil being the result of the activity of such powers within creation prior to the appearance of human beings,' Wright says.[163]

Building on this understanding, it was Karl Barth who first drew the subtle distinction between what he called *the shadow* and natural evil itself. The shadow side of nature is not evil but part of God's good creation. Thus pain and pleasure, laughter and tears, success and failure, birth and death are all part of God's original creation. God did not place humankind in the world to be cushioned from discomfort, struggle and effort, which is why God's command to men and women in Genesis 1:28 is to 'fill the earth and subdue it.'

The shadow is exactly that category of events and experiences we have already looked at, which are difficult at the time, but for which we are grateful in due course because we recognise that we have benefited from them.

Natural evil, on the other hand, never has value and is always utterly destructive. It was not created by God. It is an intruder that, through the fall of angels and then humans, has inflicted itself on the creation. Nothing good comes from it, nor can be said or thought about it. It is absolutely meaningless, irrational and cruel. It is a twisted and distorted form of the natural role that the shadow plays in the creation.

However, Wright, who holds this view, warns us that we need to distinguish wisely and carefully between the shadow and natural evil.

'From our present vantage point it may be difficult to disentangle evil from the shadow and so what belongs to either will only finally disclosed at the end, when God's purposes are fulfilled,' he says.

QUESTION TIME

1. It is difficult to reconcile the concept of a sovereign and loving God with the fact of the massive earthquake that generated the Southeast Asian tsunami killing over 280,000 people on the 26 December 2004. As a letter to one broadsheet newspaper expressed it during the following week: *'The world has found itself united in a single prayer "How could you let this happen?" Either God caused the wave to form, in which case he is malevolent, or he failed to act to stop it, in which case he is negligent.'*

How would you respond to this letter?

2. How have difficult and painful experiences in your life caused you to grow and change?

3. How would you respond if someone in your church explained to you that the reason you were suffering was because of unresolved sin in your life?

4. What is the message of the church to a world that asks, 'Why did this happen to me?'

5

Teaching Block 2: The Sovereign God: When Pain is Personal

2.1 A grief observed

Our questions about the problem of evil and suffering are not just philosophical. At some point almost everyone has cried out in their heart, if not aloud, God, why have you let this happen to me? None of us journey through life completely unscathed; a painful illness, rejection, depression, disability, betrayal, loneliness, a debilitating phobia, a broken love affair, an unhappy marriage, divorce, redundancy, the loss of a loved one. Suffering comes in many forms and they all hurt.

C.S. Lewis wrote two very different books about pain. *The Problem of Pain*, written in 1940, is the product of his brilliant and logical mind and one of the best treatments of the subject in print. *A Grief Observed*, written 21 years later, after the death of his wife from bone cancer, is very different – Lewis' confidence had been shattered:

'Meanwhile, where is God? This is one of the most disquieting symptoms. When you are happy, so happy that you have no sense of needing him, if you turn to him then with praise, you will be welcomed with open arms. But go to him when your need is desperate, when all other help is vain and what do you find? A door slammed in your face, and a sound of bolting and double bolting on the inside. After that, silence. You may as well turn away.'[164]

In the end, as we've seen, the Bible does not supply an open-and-shut text-book answer to the problem of why evil exists. For all our probing, this most painful of issues is still shrouded in some degree of mystery.

John Stott suggests that this is because the Bible's 'purpose is more practical than philosophical. Consequently, although there are references to sin and suffering on virtually every page, its concern is not to explain their origin but to help us to overcome them.'[165]

In other words, the Bible is not so much about why evil exists, though we can deduce a great deal from its pages; instead it's about how to respond to the fact of evil's existence. But the Bible does not leave us with just words, theories, or a set of abstract theological principles on how to cope.

Philip Yancey says, 'In Jesus, God gives us an up-close and personal look at his response to human suffering. All our questions about God and suffering should, in fact, be filtered through what we know about Jesus.'[166]

2.2 The vulnerable God

Jesus' life and suffering demonstrate God's solidarity with us. 'The God who allows us to suffer, once suffered himself in Christ, and continues to suffer with us and for us today,' Stott says.[167]

'For whatever reason God chose to make man as he is – limited and suffering and subject to sorrows and death – he has the honesty and courage to take his own medicine. Whatever game he is playing with his creation, he has kept his own rules and played fair … He has himself gone through the whole of human experience, from trivial irritations of family life and the cramping restrictions of hard work and lack of money to the worst horrors of pain and humiliation, defeat, despair, and death … He was born in poverty and died in disgrace and thought it well worthwhile.' (Dorothy L. Sayers)[168]

Pain is endurable, it is the seeming indifference of God that is not. However, the knowledge that God himself has endured every kind of suffering that we face makes the world of difference. God is not up there and remote – he is in here with us identifying with our pain.

'If I am caught up in terrible suffering it is one thing to be assured of the love and kindness of another person. It is quite another thing for that other person to give the assurance by entering into my situation and suffering with me or even for me. A God who empties himself out of love for human beings, who recklessly as it were gives up divine privileges to endure all the hard realities of human life, is a God whose love is credible and inspires love in return.' (Davis, Kendall and O'Collins, *Incarnation*)

The assumption that God is, first and foremost, powerful runs throughout history. Aristotle originally developed the idea that God can do anything to anyone but no-one can cause God pain. God is 'impassible' – incapable of suffering or feeling pain. The gods can affect others for good or ill yet they remain unthreatened by them – they are invulnerable.

John Stott argues, '[Unfortunately] the early Greek fathers of the church took over this notion somewhat uncritically. In consequence, their teaching about God sometimes sounds more Greek than Hebrew.'

As a result throughout much of church history this same view has been dominant. The Council of Chalcedon, for instance, dismissed the view that God could be 'passible' as 'vain babblings' and condemned all those that held it!

But during the twentieth century the theme of God's vulnerability was picked up and emphasised, primarily by German theologians – Karl Barth, Dietrich Bonhoeffer and Jürgen Moltmann. Moltmann, born in 1926, was a German prisoner of war in England in 1945, at which time he became a Christian – the interaction of these two experiences was to shape the rest of his life. In 1972 he published what was to become a hugely influential book, *The Crucified God*. In it he argues, 'A God who cannot suffer is poorer than any human. For a God who is incapable of suffering is a being who cannot be involved. Suffering and injustice do not affect him … so he is also a loveless being.'[169]

The incarnation, of course, shows us that God feels pain keenly. The shortest verse of the Bible is 'Jesus wept' (John 11:35). Jesus was not a stoic, stiff upper lip kind of man; he felt pain and sadness and expressed it as we all do, by crying. The gospel writers attribute the whole range of human emotion to Jesus, from love and compassion to anger and indignation. As the Jewish scholar Abraham Heschel[170] states, even in the Old Testament 'the most exalted idea applied to God is not infinite wisdom, infinite power, but infinite concern.'

'Impassibility is the most dubious of the divine attributes discussed in classical theism, because it suggests that God does not experience sorrow, sadness or pain. It appears to deny that God is touched by the feelings of our infirmities, despite what the Bible eloquently says about his love and his sorrow. How can God be loving and not pained by evil? How can God be impassible when the incarnate Son experienced suffering and death?' (Clark Pinnock)[171]

But God suffers as a by-product of his love. Love and pain go together. The greater the love, the greater the suffering. God, the original lover, is also the original sufferer. To have the capacity for love is to equally have the capacity for pain.

God suffers. Like a mother watching her drug addict son dissolve before her eyes, torn by the memory of his early childhood, taunted by the hopes that she once held for him and still clings to – God watches and hurts.

In fact, we have to ask ourselves, what meaning can there be in a love which is not costly to the lover? If love is self-giving, then it is inevitably vulnerable to pain, since it has to expose itself to the possibility of rejection and insult. 'In the real world of pain, how could one worship a God who was immune to it?' John Stott asks in *The Cross*.

5

The Long Silence

At the end of time, billions of people were seated on a great plain before God's throne. Most shrank back from the brilliant light before them. But some groups near the front talked heatedly, not cringing with cringing shame - but with belligerence.

'Can God judge us? How can He know about suffering?' snapped a pert young brunette. She ripped open a sleeve to reveal a tattooed number from a Nazi concentration camp. 'We endured terror ... beatings ... torture ... death!'

In another group a negro boy lowered his collar. 'What about this?' he demanded, showing an ugly rope burn. 'Lynched, for no crime but being black!'

In another crowd there was a pregnant schoolgirl with sullen eyes: 'Why should I suffer?' she murmured. 'It wasn't my fault.' Far out across the plain were hundreds of such groups. Each had a complaint against God for the evil and suffering he had permitted in his world.

How lucky God was to live in heaven, where all was sweetness and light. Where there was no weeping or fear, no hunger or hatred. What did God know of all that man had been forced to endure in this world? For God leads a pretty sheltered life, they said.

So each of these groups sent forth their leader, chosen because he had suffered the most. A Jew, a negro, a person from Hiroshima, a horribly deformed arthritic, a thalidomide child. In the centre of the vast plain, they consulted with each other. At last they were ready to present their case. It was rather clever.

Before God could be qualified to be their judge, he must endure what they had endured. Their decision was that God should be sentenced to live on earth as a man.

Let him be born a Jew. Let the legitimacy of his birth be doubted. Give him a work so difficult that even his family will think him out of his mind.

Let him be betrayed by his closest friends. Let him face false charges, be tried by a prejudiced jury and convicted by a cowardly judge. Let him be tortured.

At the last, let him see what it means to be terribly alone. Then let him die so there can be no doubt he died. Let there be a great host of witnesses to verify it.

As each leader announced his portion of the sentence, loud murmurs of approval went up from the throng of people assembled. When the last had finished pronouncing sentence, there was a long silence. No one uttered a word. No one moved.

For suddenly, all knew that God had already served his sentence.

Anon[172]

Elie Wiesel tells another story from Auschwitz. He remembers many prisoners being executed during his time in Nazi concentration camps, but none had more impact on him than the hanging of a young boy. This 'sad-eyed angel' had been a servant of one camp leader, who was trusted by the Germans. When the leader was found to have blown up the local power station, he was tortured and transferred to another camp. But the boy was also tortured, and then sentenced to hang alongside two adults. The rest of the inmates were forced to watch the execution, powerless to help.

As the three prisoners stood on the gallows, waiting to be executed, Wiesel heard a voice behind him ask, 'Where is God? Where is he?'

'Long live liberty!' the two adults cried out, in defiance of their execution. The child said nothing. The signal was given, and the three were hanged. The adults died instantly, but the boy was too light and it took more than half an hour for him to die. During this time, all the other inmates were forced to march past and look at the executed men.

As he passed the boy, still barely alive, Wiesel heard the same voice behind him ask, 'Where is God now?'

You might have expected Wiesel, who had come to doubt God's love and justice, to have asked the same question. Yet as he recalls in *Night*, 'I heard a voice within me answer him: "Where is he? Here he is – he is hanging here on this gallows"…'

What did Wiesel mean by this? Did he see in the face of the dying boy the 'man of sorrows' who 'was oppressed and afflicted, yet he did not open his mouth' (Isa 53:3,7)? Was the death of this sad-eyed angel a sign that God was suffering alongside him, or that God was equally helpless? Whatever Wiesel meant by his comment, no Christian can fail to appreciate its impact.

2.3
The suffering Servant

Moltmann goes on to talk about the cross of Christ as an 'inner-trinitarian event'. Aside from its significance for the redemption of the world it has huge impact on our understanding of God himself. At the cross both Father and Son suffer pain and anguish. Moltmann argues that the historic event of the cross shows us that God not only affects the world but is also affected by the world and above all by humankind. Through the cross, he says, we see something of the inner life of the triune God. So it is that among the answers the Bible gives to the meaning of the incarnation and cross is a most mysterious answer.

'Suffering served as a kind of 'learning experience' for God,' Yancey writes in *Where is God when it hurts?*. 'Such words seem faintly heretical, but I am merely following phraseology from the book of Hebrews … Hebrews emphasizes that Jesus 'Although he was a son, he learned obedience from what he suffered' (5:8). Elsewhere, that book tells us that the author of our salvation was made perfect through suffering (2:10). These words, full of fathomless mystery, surely mean at least this: the Incarnation had meaning for God as well as for us … Had he, a spirit, ever felt physical pain? Not until the Incarnation, the wrinkle in time when God himself experienced what it is like to be a human being … In some incomprehensible way, because of Jesus, God hears our cries differently. The author of Hebrews marvels that whatever we are going through, God has himself gone through. 'For we are not without a high priest who is unable to sympathise with our weaknesses, but we have one who has been tempted in every way, just as we are – yet was without sin' (4:15).'

In the book of Revelation, the Lion of Judah who has conquered (5:5) is revealed to be 'the Lamb who was

> Jesus reacted to personal suffering just as humanly as we do. He clearly struggled.

slaughtered'. G.B. Caird writes that it is 'as if John were saying to us ... wherever the Old Testament says Lion read Lamb.'[173] It is he who unravels the secret of history. It is the Lamb – the crucified, the stripped, the broken, the weakest of all, the God who has suffered – who presides over the last judgement.

In Jesus' life, death and resurrection we find not so much God's reasons for suffering as much as his responses to suffering. The problem of pain is not solved, or removed from our lives, but we are given an essential perspective from which to look at it and practical help in our own struggles with it.

Jesus' attitude to the suffering of others
Whenever Jesus met those who were in pain he was deeply moved – he had compassion for them. He never turned them away. He never told people to 'stop whingeing' or 'sort yourself out', to 'put a brave face on things' or to 'learn to grin and bear it.' For instance, when his friend Lazarus died, he cried as he did again over Jerusalem. He spent his whole ministry meeting people's needs and healing them of their diseases. Sometimes, in order to do so, he broke the religious taboos and social customs of the day, and as a result felt the wrath and rejection of the religious leadership for doing so.

Philip Yancey (*Where is God when it hurts?*) says, 'The patterns of Jesus' response should convince us that God is not a God who enjoys seeing us suffer.'

Jesus' attitude to his own suffering
Jesus reacted to personal suffering just as humanly as we do. He clearly struggled with it and his first response was,

on occasion, to shrink from it. For instance, in the Garden of Gethsemane he pleaded with his Father to find another, easier way rather than have to face the cross. But it was to be there that ultimately he offered us the supreme proof that God understands our suffering. It was there that God surrendered himself to pain. At one level we are all familiar with the scene so graphically portrayed in Mel Gibson's film *The Passion of The Christ*. The lonely figure hanging twisted on the cross, the nails through his hands and feet, his lacerated back, his wrenched limbs, his brow bleeding, his mouth dry, his unquenchable thirst, the soldiers laughing and spitting as he gasped for breath, the torment of suffocation, the hours of torture and public humiliation in front of the mob. But the deepest truth is this: it is here, while God hangs dying at the hands of his creatures, that at the same time, his greatest work is being accomplished.

2.4
Christ as inspiration

'Even though suffering has to be recognised as evil and therefore resisted, there nevertheless comes a time when it has to be realistically accepted,' Stott says. 'It is then that the example of Jesus, which is set before us in the New Testament for our imitation, becomes an inspiration.'

In some way, even through suffering, the Bible insists that God is at work. Though God does not always remove our pain he fills it with meaning.

An example to follow
'Christians in every generation have gained from the sufferings of Jesus ... inspiration to bear undeserved pain patiently, without either complaining or hitting back,' Stott says.

Peter tells his readers that Christ suffered for them, leaving them an example. 'Suffering is all part of the work God has given you. Christ, who suffered for you, is your example. Follow in his steps.' (1 Pet 2:21) In the words of the writer to the Hebrews, our goal is to 'fix our eyes on Jesus' for he 'endured the cross, scorning its shame'. The challenge is for us to 'consider him who endured such opposition from sinful men, so that you will not grow weary and lose heart.' (Heb 12:1-3) Suffering is seen as a normal part of the life of a follower of Christ. (Mt 5:10-12) But more than that – we are participants in Christ's suffering. Paul talks about 'sharing in his [Christ's] sufferings' so that our suffering becomes part of what it means to take up our cross and follow him. (2 Cor 1:5, Phil 3:10)

A stimulus to maturity

God uses suffering in our lives to refine us and make us more Christlike. Philip Yancey refers to this as 'transformed pain'. As we have already seen this is a paradox because although suffering, poverty and pain are bad things, yet at the same time even they, perhaps especially they, can become vehicles of God's grace.

So James wrote: 'Consider it pure joy, my brothers, whenever you face trials of many kinds, because you know that the testing of your faith develops perseverance. Perseverance must finish its work so that you may be mature and complete, not lacking anything.' (James 1:2–4)

The Bible contains a number of metaphors of this rooted in the Old Testament and developed by New Testament writers.

- The father disciplining his son. (Heb 12:5–11) Though at the time discipline is painful the result is maturity and stability for those who submit to it and are trained by it.
- The metal worker refining silver and gold. (1 Pet 1:6–7) The process is distressing, but through it our faith is purified.
- The gardener pruning his vine (John 15:1–8). The productivity of the branches depends not only on their being connected to the vine, but also on being pruned. Pruning is a drastic process – the bush has to be cut right back – but the result is fruitfulness.

A model of service

'I tell you the truth, unless a grain of wheat falls to the ground and dies, it remains only a single seed. But if it dies, it produces many seeds. The man who loves his life will lose it, while the man who hates his life in this world will keep it for eternal life. Whoever serves me must follow me … My Father will honour the one who serves me.' (John 12:23–26)

It is clear that Jesus was not only thinking of himself, but also of those who would follow him, not necessarily to martyrdom, but definitely to sacrificial, suffering service. For us as for Christ – the seed must die in order to multiply.

A pathway to joy

According to the writer to the Hebrews, Jesus endured his sufferings 'for the joy set before him.' (Heb 12:2) On the first Easter Sunday the disciples learned that no darkness was too dark for God. 'They learned what it means to judge the present by the future,' Yancey says. It may be Friday and Christ may be on the cross, but resurrection Sunday is coming! As Paul put it: 'I consider our present sufferings are not worth comparing with the glory that will be revealed in us.' (Rom 8:18)

A dependence on God

The gospels build a picture of Jesus' dependency on his Father expressed through the huge amount of time he devoted to prayer. To this end he would frequently withdraw from his followers simply to spend time with his Father. 'But Jesus often withdrew to lonely places and prayed.' (Luke 5:16) Perhaps the most significant of these occasions was in the Garden of Gethsemane just before his arrest. At his time of great suffering, just as he had throughout his life, Jesus prayed 'earnestly' and threw himself in total, though fearful, trust into his Father's arms.

QUESTION TIME

1. 'Like a mother watching her drug addict son dissolve before her eyes, torn by the memory of his early childhood, taunted by the hopes that she once held for him and still clings to – God watches and hurts.' Jesus said, 'Blessed are those who mourn.' What did he mean?

2. John 15:1–8 contains the metaphor of a gardener pruning his vine. The productivity of the branches depends not only on their being connected to the vine, but also on being pruned. Pruning is a drastic process – the bush has to be cut right back – but the result is fruitfulness. Can you think of times when you have felt pruned? What fruit did it produce?

3. Does suffering make it harder or easier to pray? Why?

5

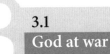

3 Teaching Block 3: The Sovereign God: The Ongoing Battle

3.1 God at war

Jesus taught his disciples to pray: 'Our Father … your kingdom come, your will be done on earth as it is in heaven.' However, we live in a world where God's will is clearly not done 'as it is in heaven'. Around 35 million people, for instance, continue to die of starvation or poverty-related diseases each and every year. These people are totally undeserving of the death sentence handed out to them simply by virtue of where they were born. No-one would deny that they are caught up as innocent victims of colossal forces, beyond their ability, indeed, perhaps beyond anyone's ability, to control.

'There are two equal and opposite errors into which our race can fall about the devils,' C.S. Lewis writes. 'One is to disbelieve in their existence. The other is to believe, and to feel an excessive and unhealthy interest in them. They themselves are equally pleased by both errors and hail a materialist or a magician with the same delight.'[174]

Christians either seem to give Satan far too much attention, ascribing to him powers of such magnitude that we almost deify him, or by contrast pay him too little heed and fall into the trap of ignoring him altogether.

In the Old Testament Satan is only specifically mentioned by name on three occasions (Zech 3:1, Job 1–2, 1 Chron 21:1). But the picture of the spiritual conflict painted in the New Testament is very different and forms such a dominant theme that scholars agree it can only be fully understood in terms of the unfolding drama between two kingdoms: that of God and that of the devil.

'Jesus' teachings were not first and foremost about high ethical ideals or profound religious insights, though they are frequently that as well. Rather, most fundamentally they are about what Jesus himself was most fundamentally about: engaging in mortal combat with the enemy of all that is godly, good and true. In his teachings we find many valuable insights into the nature of the war that ravages the earth, insights that should influence our understanding of the problem of evil.' (Gregory Boyd, *God at War*)[175]

The New Testament presents us with a world under Satan's dominion. Jesus is 'tempted by the devil' (Luke 4:1–13). He heals a woman whom Satan has 'kept bound for eighteen long years' (Luke 13:16) and is finally betrayed after Satan enters into Judas (Luke 22:3). In John's Gospel, Jesus often speaks of Satan as 'the prince of this world' (John 12:31; 14:30, 16:11) and describes him as a 'murderer' and 'the father of lies' (John 8:44). He believes himself to be in the forefront of a gigantic spiritual battle: 'How can anyone enter a strong man's house and carry off his possessions unless he first ties up the strong man?' (Matt 12:29) When he sends out his disciples to be his representatives in the towns and villages, they return excitedly to announce 'even the demons submit to us in your name.' (Luke 10:17) Jesus regards his death as the means of delivering the decisive victory through which Satan will be defeated. 'Now is the time for judgment on this world; now the prince of this world will be driven out. But I, when I am lifted up from the earth, will draw all men to myself.' (John 12:31–32)

According to Paul, who picks up on this same theme, 'having disarmed the powers and authorities, he [Jesus] made a public spectacle of them, triumphing over them by the cross.' (Col 2:15) And Peter adds that Jesus 'has gone into heaven and is at God's right hand – with angels, authorities and powers in submission to him.' (1 Pet 3:22) And 1 John 3:8 declares: 'The reason the Son of God appeared was to destroy the devil's work.' The New Testament writers are agreed – Christ's victory over Satan is decisive; the war has been won. The powers have been trodden underfoot by Jesus. The Bible does not teach the concept of dualism; that there is a battle going on between two equals – good and evil, God and the Devil – where the outcome is uncertain. Satan is a defeated enemy.

But though the cross of Christ may have been the decisive campaign in the war, and assured its final outcome, the skirmish goes on. There are battles still to fight. The Bible is realistic about the nature of the struggle. C.S. Lewis says, 'This universe is at war. But it … is a civil war, a rebellion, and we are living in a part of the universe occupied by the rebel.'[176] As Paul makes clear, our ongoing 'struggle is not against flesh and blood, but against the rulers, against the authorities, against the powers of this dark world and

> Harry Boer served four years as a chaplain during the Second World War, spending the final days of the conflict among marines in the Pacific Theatre.
>
> 'The Second Division saw much action, with great losses,' he writes. 'Yet I never met an enlisted man or an officer who doubted for a moment the outcome of the war. Nor did I ever meet a marine who asked why, if victory was so sure, we couldn't have it immediately. It was just a question of slogging through till the enemy gave up.'[177]

against the spiritual forces of evil in the heavenly realms.' (Eph 6:12) Thus he warns his readers to 'put on the full armour of God so that you can take your stand against the devil's schemes.' (Eph 6:11) God is somehow still engaged in a battle with the forces of evil, whose greatest desire is to undermine his will.

'Enemy-occupied territory – that is what this world is,' Lewis adds. 'Christianity is the story of how the rightful king has landed, you might say landed in disguise, and is calling us all to take part in a great campaign of sabotage.'

3.2. Know your enemy

The question is: What did Paul mean? If they are not 'flesh and blood', who are the 'rulers' and 'powers of this dark world'? Who are the 'spiritual forces in the heavenly realms'? Who is it we are struggling against and how do we wage the war?

- Some Christian thinkers have argued that, for Paul, the 'powers' and 'authorities' are to be wholly equated with the 'structures of earthly existence'. (Hendrik Berkof, *Christ and the Powers*, (Scottdale, Herald Press, 1962)) Paul only spoke of the battle in the 'heavenly realms' because he was reflecting and working with the culture of his day. We now realise that when the 'spirituality' of human governments, regimes, traditions, institutions, organisations and giant corporations becomes diseased it is they that become 'demonic'. For Paul, the demonic did not comprise of personal beings but simply the impersonal aspects of God's good creation gone bad. Hence the only volition that these powers have is the volition given them by people who are under them.

- Others have preferred a more traditional interpretation of Paul's phraseology, which they regard as referring literally and exclusively to angels and demons rather than social or political structures. The 'earthly structures' approach fails to take serious account of either the New Testament's witness concerning Satan and his demonic followers, or Paul's references to the spiritual conflict in the heavenly realms.

- The 'powers' are at one and the same time visible and invisible; earthly and heavenly; personal and institutional. 'The truth of the matter is that words like principalities, powers and thrones are used both of human rulers and of the spiritual forces which lie behind them,'[178] Michael Green says. Without the reality of the demonic it is difficult to understand how it is that

earthly structures become tyrannical, but conversely, it is equally difficult to grasp how Satan and his angels exercise their stranglehold if not through fallen human structures. The New Testament writers use the terms like 'authorities' and 'powers' flexibly. They refer to human authorities, which means that there is a spirituality at the heart of our political, economic and cultural structures, but they also refer to the transcendent personal demonic spirits behind those authorities.

The church is called to take the socio-political nature of

> The theologian James Stewart used Jesus' death to illustrate the interplay between the spiritual and the earthly. He identified three elements at work in the cross of Christ:
>
> - The design of human beings
> - The will of Jesus
> - The purposes of God[179]
>
> Within what he labelled 'the design of human beings' he saw a powerful coalition working together to bring Christ down. 'It was the human attitudes of pride, self-love and traditionalism and fear which, when worked out into social, political and ecclesiastical magnitudes resulted in the death of the Son of God.'[180] But behind this coalition of organised religion, Roman and Jewish politics, and popular opinion (which was easily manoeuvred and manipulated by the more unscrupulous), Stewart insisted that Satan and his hordes lurked as they orchestrated, distorted and used the human structures of the day for their own evil ends.

evil seriously without ever minimising its individual and personal aspects. Hence we are to fight systematic evil as forcefully as we are to fight individual evil.

'Inflation and unemployment, the arms race and the corruption of morals, these are all manifestations in the modern state of principalities and powers. The state does not want these things … it struggles hard to get rid of them. But it fails. It is in a grip of a power beyond its own.' (Green, *I Believe*)

'It is one thing to say that we are at war with the Devil, but where is the battlefield? This needs to be clearly located, otherwise we could be seduced into a phoney war or become embroiled in a mythic battle of our own invention. Spiritual warfare does not mean that we turn our backs on the world of everyday existence, whether it be political, economic or social…the only spiritual reality we are called to, if we wish to do battle with the Enemy, is down to earth.' (Andrew Walker, *Enemy Territory*)[181]

The evangelical withdrawal, especially in the middle part of the twentieth century, from political and social engagement was a direct outgrowth of the view that the root of all problems was the need for individual transformation.

'More recently we have been inclined to see that the changing of the individual must be accompanied by the transformation of the social context if we are to do justice to the gospel of the kingdom rather than simply one off personal salvation.' (Wright, *Dark Side*)

'Through prayer and social activism we are to labour toward exorcising the corrupted powers that structure fallen society as earnestly as we are to labour in exorcising individual demons out of individuals.' (Boyd, *War*)

3.3
What is your worldview?

Under the scientific revolution of the Enlightenment of the eighteenth century, Europe's thinkers abandoned interest in the world of the spiritual and untouchable. Empirical knowledge – the objective and verifiable world of natural processes and principles – was for them all that existed. Within this kind of worldview (or metanarrative), any talk of the devil was increasingly seen as nothing less than pure superstition.

This kind of thinking even found its way into theology, with Rudolf Bultmann claiming, 'It is impossible to use electric light and the wireless and to avail ourselves of modern medical and surgical discoveries, and at the same time to believe in the New Testament world of demons and spirits.'[182]

To some extent, even among some Christians today, the same values linger on.

'In "sophisticated" circles accounts of sexual exploits scarcely raise an eyebrow, but if you want to bring all talk to a halt in shocking embarrassment, every eye riveted on you, try mentioning angels, or demons, or the devil. You will quickly be appraised for signs of patho-logical violence and then shunned.' (Walter Wink, *Unmasking the Powers*)[183]

'We don't see the world the way that it is,' Winks says. 'We see it only the way that we perceive it to be.'[184] Our worldview (Big Story) provides the framework in which we do our thinking, the lens through which we perceive reality and make sense of our experiences. It shapes and colours the way we see things – it determines the way we think. But to make things more complicated, for most of the time a worldview functions at an unconscious level – we are not aware of its existence.

The late John Wimber, a well-known American church leader, used Acts 28:1–6 to show how influenced we are by our culture's dominant worldview. It tells how Paul, Luke and their travelling companions are shipwrecked off the island of Malta, but eventually reach land by clinging to wreckage of the boat.

'Once safely on shore … The islanders showed us unusual kindness. They built a fire and welcomed us all because it was raining and cold. Paul gathered a pile of brushwood and, as he put it on the fire, a viper, driven out by the heat, fastened itself on his hand. When the islanders saw the snake hanging from his hand, they said to each other, "This man must be a murderer; for though he escaped from the sea, Justice has not allowed him to live." But Paul shook the snake off into the fire and suffered no ill effects. The people expected him to swell up or suddenly fall dead, but after waiting a long time and seeing nothing unusual happen to him, they changed their minds and said he was a god.'

Wimber shows how the islanders were controlled by their worldview.

> **Scripture is full of examples of God's faithfulness in responding to the prayers of his people.**

- They believed in various gods, including 'Justice'. It is for this reason that the word is capitalised and turned into a personal name in Luke's text.
- They extended their 'unusual welcome' to Paul and his friends because they believed that the only possible reason they could have survived the shipwreck was if another of their gods 'Fate' was protect-ing them – therefore they must be righteous men.
- When Paul was subsequently attacked by a snake, the locals expected him to 'swell up or suddenly fall down dead' because they knew the snake was poisonous.
- As they witnessed the snake attack they revised their opinion of Paul and concluded that he 'must be a murderer; for though he escaped from the sea, Justice has not allowed him to live'.
- When Paul didn't 'swell up or suddenly fall down dead' they revised their view again; now they decided that he must also be 'a god'.

However, Wimber went on to show that our predominant Western mindset leads us to a number of different conclusions. So for modern Westerners;

'spiritual forces of evil in the heavenly realms', immediately goes on to exhort them to 'pray in the Spirit on all occasions with all kinds of prayers and requests.' (Eph 6:18)

The belief that prayer makes a difference and significantly influences the outcome of events is central to the Bible – both the Old and New Testaments. Scripture is full of examples of God's faithfulness in responding to the prayers of his people. For example, there are many instances where the Bible directly states that God intended to bring judgment on people or a city but reversed his course of action in the light of prayer (e.g., Exod 32:14; Num 11:1–2; 14:12–20; 16:20–35; Deut 9:13–14, 18–20, 25; 2 Sam 24:17–25; 1 Kings 21:27–29; 2 Chron 12:5–8; Jer 26:19). In fact, one of the most fundamental assumptions running throughout Scripture is that 'the prayer of the righteous is powerful and effective.' (James 5:16)

Jesus frequently taught on the importance of prayer. He repeatedly instructed his disciples to ask God for what they wanted, promising it would be given to them (Matt 7:7,11; 18:19–20; John 14:13–16; 15:7,16; 16:23). And he also encouraged them to pray with persistence – not taking 'no' for an answer (Luke 11:5–13; 18:1–8). None of this teaching makes any sense if prayer does not actually change things and cause God to bring about a state of affairs that otherwise would not have occurred. In fact, unless it does it is difficult, if not impossible, to explain the urgency that the Bible attributes to the need for intercession.

- The reason Paul and friends survived the storm was because the wind and tide were in their favour and they were strong swimmers.
- The reason that Paul didn't 'swell up or suddenly fall down dead' following the snake attack was either because the snake was an old one, or because it had just bitten someone else and had no venom left, or because, in the light of the fire, the locals made a mistake and mistook it for a more dangerous species.

Wimber concluded by explaining that neither worldview – ours or that of the first century inhabitants of Malta – is biblical and both need to be recalibrated by Scripture.

3.4
The power of prayer

'Our spiritual struggle must therefore be carried on simultaneously on two fronts: Through prayer and persuasive action … in persuasive action men and women and institutions are called to invest in what is good and true rather than what is false … In prayer the power of the kingdom of God is given access to human life.' (Wright, *Dark Side*)

Jesus taught his disciples to pray that God's kingdom will come, and Paul, having reminded the Ephesians that their struggle was against 'rulers,' 'authorities,' 'powers' and

'God has of his own motion placed himself under the law of prayer, and has obligated himself to answer the prayers of men. He has ordained prayer as a means whereby he will do things through men as they pray, which he would not otherwise do…,' E.M. Bounds says. 'If prayer puts God to work on earth, then, by the same token, prayerlessness rules God out of the world's affairs, and prevents him from working.'[185]

Elsewhere he adds, 'The driving power, the conquering force in God's cause is God himself. 'Call on me and I will answer thee and show thee great and mighty things which though knowest not,' is God's challenge to prayer. Prayer puts God in full force into God's work.'[186]

So what difference does prayer make? If God is good and knows our needs anyway – why bother to pray?

Some claim that prayer is primarily for our benefit, not God's. Prayer does not change God, but it is the means by which God changes us.

'When I speak of moving God, I do not mean that God's mind is changed by prayer, or that his disposition or character is changed. But prayer produces such a change in us as renders it consistent for God to do as it would not be consistent for him to do otherwise.' (Charles Finney, *Revival Lectures*)[187]

Prayer is a valuable reminder to us of our dependence on God. 'Prayer is not so much an act as it is an attitude – an attitude of dependency, dependency upon God.' (A.W. Pink, *The Sovereignty of God*)[188]

Prayer is God's chosen means by which he brings about his pre-ordained ends. 'Prayer is not a convenient device for imposing our will upon God, or bending his will to ours, but the prescribed way of subordinating our will to his.' (John Stott, *The Letters of John*)[189]

Whilst each of these perspectives clearly contains some truth about the gift of prayer, any straightforward reading of scripture would seem to indicate that the impact of believing prayer is more than this. We must obviously always be wary of falling into the belief that, in some way, prayer is about asking God for what we want, and then expecting him to supply it – reducing him to a servant, there simply to do our bidding and grant our desires. However, in one of the most curious incidents in Jesus' ministry he caused a fig tree to wither and die. But when his disciples asked how it happened, Jesus replied, 'I tell you the truth, if you have faith and do not doubt, not only can you do what was done to the fig tree, but also you can say to this mountain, "Go, throw yourself into the sea," and it will be done. If you believe, you will receive whatever you ask for in prayer.' (Matt 21:21–22)

> **"Now the dwelling of God is with men, and he will live with them. They will be his people, and God himself will be with them."**

And once again, James 5:15 echoes a similar message: 'The prayer offered in faith will make the sick person well; the Lord will raise him up.'

'Unless it is sometimes true that God brings about the course of events in a way that he would not had he not been asked, petitionary prayer is idle: just as it would be idle for a boy to ask his father for a specific birthday present if the father has made up his mind what to give irrespective of what the boy asks.' (Peter Geach, *Providence and Evil*)[190]

If we understand that we are on a battlefield – where God's will is not always seen but where Jesus calls us to pray and work so that one day it will be done 'as it is in heaven'; if we understand that as soldiers of the cross we are called to 'put on the full armour of God so that [we] can take [our] stand against the devil's schemes' (Eph 6:11); then our prayers will sustain our relationship with God; they will shape us to be more like him – to understand more of his will and purposes – but we will be ready for hardship, setbacks and disappointments. 'Therefore put on the full armour of God, so that when the day of evil comes, you may be able to stand your ground, and after you have done everything, to stand.' (Eph 6:13)

Writing to the church in Rome, Paul encourages his friends.

'Who shall separate us from the love of Christ? Shall trouble or hardship or persecution or famine or nakedness or danger or sword? … For I am convinced that neither death nor life, neither angels nor demons, neither the present nor the future, nor any powers, neither height nor depth, nor anything else in all creation, will be able to separate us from the love of God that is in Christ Jesus our Lord.' (Rom 8:35, 38–39)

While Paul clearly teaches that we are to 'pray in the Spirit on all occasions', he obviously assumes that 'trouble … hardship … persecution … famine … nakedness … danger … sword …[and] death' not only can, but do happen to Christians. Thus his encouragement for the Romans is not that these things cannot, or will not, happen to them but that even when they do happen they cannot separate them from the love of Christ. Or, as Gregory Boyd puts it, 'We pray for protection and believe that prayer is "powerful and effective" (James 5:16), but we still lock our doors at night.'

Scripture points beyond our present struggles to God's ultimate victory in which we will share.

'Then I saw a new heaven and a new earth, for the first heaven and the first earth had passed away, and there was no longer any sea. I saw the Holy City, the new Jerusalem, coming down out of heaven from God, prepared as a bride beautifully dressed for her husband. And I heard a loud voice from the throne saying, "Now the dwelling of God is with men, and he will live with them. They will be his people, and God himself will be with them and be their God. He will wipe every tear from their eyes. There will be no more death or mourning or crying or pain, for the old order of things has passed away."' (Rev 21:1–4)

Our God is the Sovereign God!

QUESTION TIME

1. Name some of the big institutions and forces, beyond any individual's control, which impinge on our lives and shape our world? How do they influence us?

2. If the 'powers of this dark world' are taken on when a young married couple move into a community without a church, to live there and start one: what other examples can you think of? In your community what are the evils that you need to struggle against (a) in your life? (b) in the life of your church? (c) in the life of the church in the world?

3. 'If your God always comes to your rescue and gets you out of trouble,' the teacher would tell his students, 'it is time you started searching for the true God.' When asked to elaborate, this is the story he told: 'A man left a brand-new bicycle unattended at the marketplace while he went about his shopping. He only remembered the bicycle the following day – and rushed to the marketplace, expecting it would have been stolen. The bicycle was exactly where he had left it. Overwhelmed with joy, he rushed to a nearby church to thank God for having kept his bicycle safe only to find, when he got out, that the bicycle was gone.' Why is this?

4. Pray these words together and reflect on them. What do they say to you?

'Our Father, who is in heaven; hallowed be your name; your kingdom come; your will be done on earth as it is in heaven. Give us this day our daily bread; and forgive us our sins as we forgive those who sin against us, and lead us not into temptation; but deliver us from evil.'

FURTHER READING

Where is God when it Hurts? by Philip Yancey (Zondervan, 1977) is a compelling study of the nature of pain, God and suffering.

The Problem of Pain by C.S. Lewis (HarperCollins, 1944) is a fiercely logical treatment of the question 'Why does God allow suffering?'

A Grief Observed also by C.S. Lewis (HarperCollins, 1961) is, in contrast, a deeply moving and personal account of his grief following his wife's death from cancer.

Why Forgive? by Johann Christoph Arnold (Plough, 2000) is an incredibly poignant collection of stories about the power of forgiveness.

Red Moon Rising by Pete Greig and Dave Roberts (Kingsway, 2004) tells the story of the 24/7 Prayer movement. It is a timely reminder of the power of prayer.

Endnotes

1   Douglas Coupland, *Life After God,* (London: Simon and Schuster, 1994)

2   Richard Dawkins, *River out of Eden: A Darwinian View of Life*, (HarperCollins, 1995), p. 133

3   William Lane & Quentin Smith, *Theism, Atheism and Big Bang Cosmology*, (Oxford: Clarendon Press, 1993)

4   Michael Lloyd, *Café Theology*, (London: Alpha International, 2005)

5   Bill Bryson, *A Short History of Nearly Everything*, (London: Black Swan, 2004)

6   Stephen Hawking, *The Beginning of Time*, (http://www. hawking.org.uk/lectures/lindex.html)

7   David Wilkinson, *God, The Big Bang and Stephen Hawking*, (Crowborough: Monarch, 1996)

8   Wilkinson, *Big Bang*

9   Wilkinson, *Big Bang*

10 Ernest Lucas, *Can we Believe in Genesis Today?* (Leicester: IVP, 2001)

11 David Field and Peter Toon, *Real Questions*, (Tring: Lion, 1982)

12 William A Dembski *The Design Revolution: answering the toughest questions about intelligent design,* (Leicester: Inter-Varsity Press, 2004)

13 Albert Einstein, quoted in 'Wit & Wisdom', *The Week*, 13 November 2004

14 Colin Gunton, *The Christian Faith,* (Oxford: Blackwell, 2002)

15 Judy Pearsall (ed), *The Concise Oxford Dictionary*, (Oxford: Oxford University Press, 1999)

16 David Wilkinson, *BST The Message of Creation* (Leicester: Inter-Varsity Press, 2002)

17 Roger Forster, *Trinity*, (Milton Keynes: Authentic, 2004)

18 Forster, *Trinity*

19 Nigel Wright, *The Theology of the Dark Side*, (Carlisle: Paternoster, 2003)

20 Jim Packer, *Knowing God*, (London: Hodder and Stoughton, 1993)

21 Packer, *Knowing*

22 Packer, *Knowing*

23 Lloyd, *Café*

24 Wright, *Dark Side*

25 Copyright © Rob Lacey 2005 (Genesis 1 from *the word on the street* with a creative reflection by Rob Lacey. For permission to use please contact roblacey@thewordonthestreet.co.uk)

26 Gunton, *Christian Faith*

27 Lloyd, *Café*

28 Conrad Hyers, 'Biblical Literalism: Constricting the Cosmic Dance' in Roland Mushat Frye (ed.), *Is God a Creationist? The Religious Case Against Creation-Science*, (New York: Scribner's, 1983)

29 Wilkinson, *Creation*

30 Wikipedia article, Beetle, (http://en.wikipedia.org/wiki/ Beetle)

31 Pearsall, *Concise*

32 Wilkinson, *Creation*

33 Stanley Grenz, *The Social God and the Relational Self,* (London: Westminster John Knox, 2001)

34 Howard Peskett & Vinoth Ramachandra, *BST The Message of Mission*, (Leicester: IVP, 2003)

35 cited in C. Everett Koop, *The Right to Live, the Right to Die,* (Carol Stream: Tyndale, 1976)

36 Thomas Aquinas, *Summa Theologica* 1.75.5

37 Aquinas, *Summa*, I/II.113.10

38 Aquinas, *Summa*, III.23.1

39 Augustine, *On the Trinity*, 14.8.11

40 Grenz, *Social*

41 Claus Westermann, *Genesis 1-11: A Commentary*, Tras. John Scullion (London: SPCK)

42 Westermann, *Genesis*

43 Westermann, *Genesis*

44 Grenz, *Social,* citing Werner Schmidt, *Die Schopfungsgeschichte der Priesterschrift*, (Neukirchen-Vluyn: Neukirchener Verlag, 1964)

45 D.J.A. Clines, "The Image of God in Man," *Tyndale Bulletin* 19 (1968)

46 Gerhard von Rad, *Genesis: A Commentary*, trans. John Marks (Philadelphia: Westminster, 1973)

47 Grenz, *Social*

48 Clines, *Image*

49 Gordon Wenham, *Genesis 1-15*, vol. 1 of the *Word Biblical Commentary*, ed. David A. Hubbard, Glenn W. Barker and John D. W. Watts (Waco: Word, 1987)

50 Peskett & Ramachandra, *Mission*

51 Peskett & Ramachandra, *Mission*

52 Phyllis Bird, "'Male and Female He Created Them': Genesis 1:27b in the Context of the Priestly Account of Creation," *Harvard Theological Review* 74 (1981)

53 Jürgen Moltmann, *God in Creation: A New Theology of Creation and the Spirit of God*, trans. Margaret Kohl (San Francisco: Harper & Row, 1985)

54 Clines, *Image*

55 Ronald J. Sider, 'Biblical Foundations for Creation Care' in R.J. Berry (ed.), *The Care of Creation* (Leicester: IVP, 2000)

56 von Rad, *Genesis*

57 Wenham, *Genesis*

58 Peskett & Ramachandra, *Mission*

59 cited in Berry, *Care*

60 cited in Koop, *Right*

61 http://news.bbc.co.uk/1/hi/england/2036865.stm and http:// www.royal.gov.uk/output/Page1396.asp

62 Polly Toynbee, 'In the name of God', *The Guardian*, Friday July 22, 2005

63 Michael Frost & Alan Hirsh, *The Shaping of Things to Come*, (Peabody: Hendrickson, 2003)

64 Ruth Jenkins, *The Emergence and Development of Yahwism within its Ancient Near Eastern Environment*, (Unpublished undergraduate dissertation)

65 Jean-François Lyotard, *The Postmodern Condition: A Report on Knowledge* (Minneapolis: University of Minnesota Press, 1984) Translated by Geoff Bennington and Brian Massumi

66 David Smith, *Mission After Christendom* (London: Darton, Longman & Todd, 2003)

67 Smith, *Mission*, quoting John Berger

68 Vincent Donovan, *Christianity Rediscovered* (London: SCM Press, 1982)

69 Harold Netland, *Dissonant Voices: Religious pluralism and the Question of Truth* (Leicester: Inter-Varsity Press, 1991)

70 Peter G. Riddell, *Christians and Muslims*, (Leicester: Inter-Varsity Press, 2002)

71 William Carey, *An Enquiry into the Obligations of Christians to use Means for the Conversion of the Heathens* (Baptist Missionary Society, 1792)

72 Smith, *Mission*, quoting Hilaire Belloc

73 John Hick, *God Has Many Names*, (London: Macmillan, 1980)

74 Ken Gnanakan, *The Pluralistic Predicament*, (Bangalore: Theological Book Trust, 1992) citing Lesslie Newbigin, *The Gospel in a Pluralistic Society*, (London: SPCK, 1989)

75 Gnanakan, *Pluralistic* citing Newbigin, *Gospel*

76 Gnanakan, *Pluralistic*

77 Gnanakan, *Pluralistic*

78 http://www.lausanne.org/Brix?pageID=12898

79 Raymond Panikkar, *The Unknown Christ of Hinduism*, (London: Darton, Longman & Todd, 1964)

80 Peter Cotterell, *Mission and Meaninglessness: The good news in a world of suffering and disorder*, (London: SPCK, 1990)

81 Smith, *Mission*, quoting Constance Padwick

82 Clark Pinnock, 'An Inclusivist View' in Okholm & Phillips, *Four Views*

83 Gnanakan, *Pluralistic* citing Newbigin, *Gospel*

84 Jim Packer, *God's Words*, (Leicester: Inter-Varsity Press, 1981)

85 David Edwards and John Stott, *Essentials*, (London: Hodder and Stoughton, 1988)

86 Gnanakan, *Pluralistic*, citing Martin Goldsmith, *What about other Faiths?* (London: Hodder and Stoughton, 1989)

87 Lesslie Newbigin, *The Gospel in a Pluralistic Society*, (London: SPCK, 1989)

88 Riddell, *Christians*

89 Newbigin, *Gospel*

90 Lesslie Newbigin, Lamin Sanneh & Jenny Taylor, *Faith and Power: Christianity in Secular Britain*, (Eugene: Wipf & Stock, 2005)

91 Newbigin, Sanneh & Taylor, *Faith*

92 Newbigin, Sanneh & Taylor, *Faith*

93 Newbigin, Sanneh & Taylor, *Faith*

94 Andrew Walls, *The Cross-Cultural Process in Christian History*, (Edinburgh: T & T Clark, 2002)

95 Walls, *Cross-Cultural*

96 Walls, *Cross-Cultural*

97 Smith, *Mission*

98 Smith, *Mission*

99 Smith, *Mission*

100 E.P.T Crampton, *Christianity in Northern Nigeria*, (New York: Macmillan, 1975)

101 Smith, *Mission*

102 Smith, *Mission*

103 David Lyons, *Religion and Globalisation* (2002)

104 Peskett & Ramachandra, *Mission*, citing Address to the Canadian Senate and the House of Commons in Ottawa, 29 April 1999, "Kosovo and the end of the Nation State", *The New York Review of Books*, 10 June 1999.

105 Dan Brown, *The Da Vinci Code*, (London: Corgi, 2004)

106 Wolfhart Pannenberg, *Jesus – God and Man*, trans. Lewis Wilkins and Duane Priebe, (London: SCM, 1968)

107 Lloyd, *Café*

108 Gerald O'Collins, 'The Critical Issues' in Stephen Davis, Daniel Kendall & Gerald O'Collins (eds.), *The Incarnation*, (Oxford: Oxford University Press, 2002)

109 Lloyd, *Café*

110 I. Howard Marshall, *The Origins of New Testament Christology*, (Leicester: Inter-Varsity Press, 1976)

111 N.T. Wright, 'Jesus' Self-Understanding' in Davis, Kendall, O'Collins, *Incarnation*

112 Pannenberg, *Jesus*

113 N.T. Wright, *Jesus and the Victory of God* (London: SPCK, 1996)

114 Marshall, *Origins*

115 Marshall, *Origins*

116 Marshall, *Origins*

117 Graham Stanton, 'Message and Miracles', in Markus Bockmuehl (ed.), *The Cambridge Companion to Jesus*, (Cambridge: Cambridge University Press, 2001)

118 Graham McFarlane, *Why Do You Believe What You Believe About Jesus?* (Carlise: Paternoster Press, 2000)

119 Stephen T. Davis, 'Was Jesus Mad, Bad or God?' in Davis, Kendall, O'Collins, *Incarnation*

120 cited in N.T. Wright, *Jesus and the Victory of God*, (London: SPCK, 1996)

121 Graham McFarlane, *Why Do You Believe What You Believe About the Holy Spirit?* (Carlisle: Paternoster Press, 1998)

122 McFarlane, *Jesus*

123 Davis, Kendall, O'Collins, *Incarnation*, citing Justin Martyr, *Dialogue with Trypho*

124 A.E. Harvey, 'Christ as Agent' in L.D. Hurst & N.T. Wright (eds), *The Glory of Christ in the New Testament*, (Oxford: Clarendon Press, 1987)

125 Roger E. Olsen & Christopher A. Hall, *The Trinity*, (Grand Rapids: Eerdmans, 2002)

126 Donald Macleod, *The Person of Christ*, (Downers Grove: Inter-Varsity Press, 1998)

127 Geoffrey Wainwright, 'The Holy Spirit', in Colin Gunton (ed), *The Cambridge Companion to Christian Doctrine*, (Cambridge: Cambridge University Press, 1997)

128 Nicene-Constantinopolitan Creed

129 Derek Tidball, *BST The Message of the Cross*, (Leicester: Inter-Varsity Press, 2001)

130 Paul Tillich, *A History of Christian Thought: From its Judaic and Hellenistic Origins to Existentialism,* Carl Braaten (ed), (New York: Simon and Schuster, 1968)

131 Leonardo Boff, *Trinity and Society,* trans. Paul Burns (Maryknoll: Orbis, 1998)

132 Gordon Mursell (ed.), *The Story of Christian Spirituality,* (Tring: Lion, 2001)

133 John Donne "Meditation XVII" of *Devotions Upon Emergent Occasions*

134 A.J. Conyers, *God, Hope, and History,* (Macon: Mercer Press, 1988)

135 Miroslav, *After Our Likeness: the Church as the Image of the Trinity,* (Grand Rapids: Eerdmans, 1998) citing Joseph Ratzinger, *Theologische Prinzipienlehre: Bausteine zur Fundamentaltheologie,* (Munich: Erich Wewel, 1982)

136 Volf, *After,* citing Joseph Ratzinger, *Auf Christus Schauen: Einübung in Glaube, Hoffnung, Liebe,* (Frieburg: Herder, 1989)

137 Volf, *After,* citing John Zizioulas, *Being as Communion: Studies in Personhood and the Church,* (Crestwood: St. Vladimir's Seminary Press, 1985)

138 John Stott, *The Cross of Christ,* (Leicester: Inter-Varsity Press, 1986)

139 Lesslie Newbigin, *Discovering Truth in a Challenging World,* (London: Alpha International, 2003)

141 Johann Christoph Arnold, *Why Forgive?* (Robertsbridge: The Plough, 2000)

142 Arnold, *Why,* quoting Aleksandr Solzhenitsyn

143 C.S. Lewis, *Mere Christianity,* (London: Fontana, 1952)

144 Arnold, *Why*

145 Arnold, *Why,* citing Martin Luther King, *Strength to Love,* (Minneapolis: Augsburg Fortress, 1963)

146 M. Scott Peck, *The Road Less Travelled,* (London: Arrow, 1990)

147 Walter Wink, *Engaging the Powers,* (Minneapolis: Fortress Press, 1992)

148 Jim Wallis, *The Soul of Politics,* (Maryknoll: Orbis, 1994)

149 cited in Arnold, *Why*

150 Elie Wiesel, *Night,* Trans. S. Rodway, (Harmondsworth: Penguin, 1981)

151 Stott, *The Cross*

152 Fyodor Dostoevsky, *The Dream of a Ridiculous Man,* Trans. Alan Myers (Oxford: Oxford University Press, 1999)

153 Wright, *Dark Side*

154 C.S. Lewis, *The Problem of Pain,* (New York: Macmillan, 1944)

155 John Stuart Mill, *Nature and Utility of Religion* (New York: Macmillan, 1958)

156 Philip Yancey, *Where is God When it Hurts?* (Grand Rapids: Zondervan, 1990)

157 Lewis, *Pain*

158 Stott, *The Cross*

159 Wright, *Dark Side*

160 John Calvin, *The Institutes of the Christian Religion,* Trans. Ford Lewis Battles (London: Westminster John Knox, 2001)

161 Wright, *Dark Side*

162 Bruce Milne, *Know the Truth: Handbook of Christian Belief,* (Leicester: Inter-Varsity Press, 1998)

163 Wright, *Dark Side*

164 C.S. Lewis, *A Grief Observed,* (New York: HarperCollins, 1961)

165 Stott, *The Cross*

166 Yancey, *Where*

167 Stott, *The Cross*

168 Dorothy L. Sayers, *Christian Letters to a Post-Christian World,* (Grand Rapids: Eerdmans, 1969)

169 Jürgen Moltmann, *The Crucified God,* (Minneapolis: Augsburg Fortress, 1993)

170 cited in Stott, *The Cross*

171 Clark Pinnock, 'Systematic Theology' in Clark Pinnock, Richard Rice, John Sanders, William Hasker and David Basinger, *The Openness of God* (Downers Grove: Inter Varsity Press 1994)

172 http://www.ldolphin.org/silence.html

173 G.B. Caird, *The Revelation of Saint John,* (Peabody: Hendrickson, 1993)

174 C.S. Lewis, *The Screwtape Letters,* (London: Fount, 1942)

175 Gregory Boyd, *God at War,* (Downers Grove: IVP, 1997)

176 Lewis, *Mere Christianity*

177 cited in Yancey, *Where*

178 Michael Green, *I believe in Satan's Downfall,* (London: Hodder & Stoughton, 1981)

179 cited in Wright, *Dark Side*

180 James Stewart, 'On a neglected emphasis in New Testament Theology', *Scottish Journal of Theology* 4 (1951)

181 Andrew Walker, *Enemy Territory: The Christian Struggle for the Modern World,* (London: Hodder & Stoughton, 1987)

182 Rudolf Bultmann *et al, Kerygma and Myth,* (New York: Harper Torchbooks, 1961)

183 Walter Wink, *Unmasking the Powers,* (Philadelphia: Fortress Press, 1986)

184 Walter Wink, *The Powers that Be: Theology for a New Millennium,* (New York: Doubleday 1998)

185 E.M. Bounds, *The Weapon of Prayer,* (New Kensington: Whitaker, 1996) http://www.fbinstitute.com/Bounds/Weapon_of_Prayer_Text.html

186 E.M. Bounds, *Purpose in Prayer,* (Grand Rapids: Christian Classics Ethereal Library, 2001) http://www.ccel.org/ccel/bounds/purpose.html

187 Charles G. Finney, *Revival Lectures (Lecture 4),* (New Jersey: Fleming H Revell Co., 1993)

188 A.W. Pink, *The Sovereignty of God,* (Edinburgh: Banner of Truth, 1961)

189 John Stott, *The Letters of John,* (Grand Rapids: Eerdmans, 1988)

190 Gregory Boyd, *Satan and the Problem of Evil,* (Downers Grove: IVP, 2001) citing Peter Geach, *Providence and Evil,* (Cambridge: Cambridge University Press, 1977)